Esquire's
WORLD OF GOLF

STAFF

LEWIS W. GILLENSON, Editor-in-Chief
PHILIP DOYLE, Associate Editor
BRENDAN WOOD, Director of Production
CHARLES VAXER, Production Associate
CHARLES FORNARA, Director of Manufacturing
SALLY WEINSTOCK, Assistant Editor

Esquire's

WORLD
OF
GOLF

What Every Golfer Must Know

By Herb Graffis
Foreword by Tommy Armour and Sam Snead
Original illustrations by Lealand Gustavson

Published by Esquire, Inc., New York
in association with
Trident Press, New York

CONTENTS

PREFACE

by Sam Snead and Tommy Armour

BY SAM SNEAD

Herb Graffis has been the writing caddie for many expert golfers who wanted an expert at translating their golfing brains and muscles into type. In all the times and all the places he has been on this job a flock of the right answers must have rubbed off and into his book.

I am sure that he has as much fun out of golf as anybody alive even when he does hit his share of unfunny shots. He was a champion at enjoying golf and helping others enjoy it when I was a lad breaking into the championships. He still is getting more laughs out of golf than most all of the amateurs and the three-putting professionals.

BY TOMMY ARMOUR

A book written by Herb Graffis on how to enjoy golf is the production of an authority. No one has more fun at golf than he does. I have had the good fortune to collaborate in a lot of the merriment he has had in golf and has contributed to the game. He says I have taught him a great deal about getting the most of living out of golf. He always has been an apt student.

Whether a Graffis shot is deliberately good, accidentally satisfactory or one that should make him blush he makes the shot score for him in the pursuit of happiness.

His book makes sense for the golfer who wants to play well but, primarily, play.

Tommy Armour

WHAT
IS
THERE
TO
LEARN?

When you go through the hundreds of pages that Esquire has printed on the subject of hitting a small ball into a larger hole, you begin to sense the basic simplicity of golf.

There really hasn't been a whole lot of change in the technique of taking a swipe at the ball then rolling it into the hole since the first golf book on golf instruction was published in 1857. The writer must have had a hunch of what he was starting. He didn't sign his real name, H. B. Farnie. "A Keen Hand" was his nom de plume on his book, "The Golfer's Manual," which began the printed search to find golf's "secret."

From Bob Jones to Arnold Palmer the roster of Esquire's contributing champions lists stars who could be designated the research experts of golf. None of them were "natural" golfers, if there is such a thing. They had to think themselves to the top.

BRAIN POWER

Jones' game developed with brain power. Ben Hogan studied and worked on his golf like an atomic scientist applying himself to his job. Tommy Armour says he has taken more golf lessons than anyone else he has known. Arnold Palmer never got far in the National Amateur championship until he won it in 1954. Then he had to go 39 holes in a semi-final match to beat Eddie Meister then defeated Bob Sweeney on the last hole. But after that, turning pro, Palmer really began learning. Cary Middle-coff wasn't brilliant as an amateur; neither was Horton Smith. When they became professionals — which meant having to think every shot or lose money — they learned a lot about golf. Lawson Little and Bobby Locke were brilliant amateurs who took successful post-graduate courses as pros.

Johnny Revolta, Johnny Farrell, Claude Harmon, Jimmy Thomson, Jimmy Demaret, Vic Ghezzi, Toney Penna, Al Ciuci and others whose learning passed the test of competitive play, and Alex Morrison, Frank Walsh, Eddie Loos, Joe Novak and others who became conspicuously successful as teachers, also are among the Esquire authorities whose lessons have been screened for this summation.

DEVIATIONS

There aren't irreconcilable deviations in the testimony. The cynics who ask why the pros don't get together in telling what they know about playing golf haven't read the golf gospel according to its foremost evangelists. The game's preachers, like the scriptural prophets, have said substantially the same thing but from different temperamental viewpoints. A scholarly golfer who en-joys being bothered might give deep study to what Ben Hogan has to say about having the right foot at a right angle to the direction line at address and what Tommy Armour advises about having the right foot toed out a trifle. Theologians have worried about similar minor differences in testimony and teaching of Matthew, Mark, Luke and John on more important subjects than golf but in all cases, old and new, the right answer is deter-mined by experience of the lowly one who is seeking the solution of the mysteries.

What makes the search eternally tough is that there

is no "secret." The nearest any star of playing or teaching gets to a "secret" is a key position or movement that seems to provide him with a primary element of control in making the shot. That key differs in individuals. The great players and tutors and the ordinary golfer each have two feet, legs, hands and arms, one body and one head, so, theoretically, they all ought to operate about the same. But when one fellow thinks that when his left shoulder is working a certain way he has golf licked another is convinced that he always plays well when he points his chin to the right of the ball in taking

3

his stance and keeps it there until he's hit his shot. And so on through an army of golfers; great, medium and awful. What the multitude of masterly articles on golf add up to is giving you a wide selection of helpful directives, some of which may be exactly right for exactly the kind of guy you are.

Business men spend less time in the office than golf pros spend on the course.

A trouble with golf as a playful pastime is that it is played by athletically adept people, clumsy people and a great many men in the middle who have to make a living before they can get around to playing golf. What the average businessman golfer may not realize is that the exceptionally good golfer may have good coordination that gives him an advantage in learning the game and

4

may spend hour after hour playing and practicing. Fellows like Hogan and Snead, Palmer, Nicklaus, Nichols, Venturi, Casper and Lema usually play and practice golf more hours per week than the typical office executive or worker spends weekly on his job.

Yet, as much as the experts work on becoming supermen, they still have moments when they slump back to being merely mortals who miss shots your old Aunt Emma could — and does — make. So be of good cheer and hope eternal.

Just one little thing — and only the Good Lord or the Devil himself knows what it is — may go wrong in a golf shot, then there is misery. Bob Jones brought that out in an interview Ed Miles did for Esquire not long after Bob had retired from competition and was reminiscing. He told Miles that at Merion in 1916 as a kid of 14 and playing in his first National Amateur championship, he got 74 on the West course in the morning, led the field on that 18 of Merion, then took an 89 in the afternoon on the East course, to qualify with 163. That 15 strokes difference jolted young Jones. Bob recalled:

"I learned what all golfers learn in important play . . . you may feel your best and swing with confidence that the shot will be good but somewhere in the course of the swing the mechanics slip. It may be the merest trifle of a slip but it spoils your timing and control. To your surprise the shot turns out badly."

Maybe someone will come along and win more major national championships than the 13 Jones won, including the sweep of the U. S. and British Open and Amateur championships in 1930. The professionals are trying hard, with the Masters and the Professional Golfers Association championships substituted for the two national Amateur events, but haven't been getting close to the One and Only. If a triumphant successor does come into golf and ends discussions about who's "greatest," Jones, Hagen, Hogan, Palmer or your own sentimental choice, he will have to be magnificently extraordinary to outrank Jones as the most scholarly of the outstanding golfers. Jones as a law student and in practice as a corporation lawyer has been the sort of a champion he's been on golf courses.

Palaver about Jones pops up often in this book. Most of the references will indicate that there's not any fundamental difference between Jones and Jack Nicklaus, the brilliant young man some say will be as great as Jones. The French explained the similarity, probably, when referring to another grand game: "Plus ça change, plus c'est la même chose;" the more it changes, the more it is the same thing.

Jones selected as professional at Atlanta's East Lake Country Club — the club that was his home in golf — a studious and capable English-born American named George Sargent.

Sargent had been assistant to Harry Vardon in England. When he came to the United States he blossomed as a player. He won the United States Open in 1909 and the Canadian Open in 1912. Before Jones got him for East Lake Sargent had been professional at Hyde Manor, Chevvy Chase, Interlachen, Inverness and Scioto.

EARLY STYLES

As the first head of the Professional Golfers Association Teaching committee Sargent made slow motion pictures of the swings of Jones, Hagen, Vardon and Joyce Wethered, queen of the English girl golfers. Those pictures had much to do with determining today's American playing and teaching styles.

Sargent maintained that there had been only four

important developments in methods made in golf since golf had started and all of them were made in the past century. He declared that anybody who could apply these four significant improvements would be an exceptionally good golfer.

The Basic Basics. The four fundamentals of good golf form, according to Sargent, are:
(1) The steady head;
(2) Proficiency in handling the club;
(3) The straight left arm;
(4) The close-in right elbow.

That's all the golf shotmaking technique you need to know, according to the way Sargent, a very successful teacher, looked at the game. His view was slightly more complicated than that of another highly successful teacher, Ernest Jones, who demonstrated that if you simply learned how to swing the club and had the ball at address so it would be in the correct place to have your swing connect, you'd play good golf.

You'll read much in this book about the Sargent discoveries. Ben Hogan, plainly the greatest player of his time, and a thoughtful student and teacher, wrote Esquire articles, in which the hand action and the close-in right elbow observations of Sargent were accented.

Sargent told of the history of the four principal advances in golf methods. He started with young Tom Morris who, in 1868, won the ninth British Open Championship. His father had won the second one, in 1861, and repeated in 1862, 1864 and 1867. Young Tom made a discovery that made him champion in 1868, 1869 and 1870 when The Belt was the symbol of the championship. None of the canny Scots thought The Belt would be won in three consecutive years so when the unexpected happened and The Belt became the property of

Young **TOM MORRIS** and **THE BELT**, symbol of the British Open Championship, which he retired after three consecutive wins in **1868~1869~1870.**

young Tom, the British Open championship was discontinued. It was renewed in 1872, after a year's lapse, and the junior Morris won the present championship cup for the first time. His score in 1872 soared to 166 at Prestwick from his 149 on the same course in 1870. Prestwick then was 12 rugged holes. They had to be played three times for the 36 holes which were the British Open test until 1891.

A Good Golf Head: Steady. Anybody who could play wild and narrow Prestwick three times in 149 must have had something the rest of them didn't have and which is still good today.

STEADY HEAD BALANCE

What young Tom Morris had was balance and what gave him that was keeping his head steady, said the analytical Sargent. With the steady head serving as the hub of the axis of the swing there was introduced into golf an

Tom Morris proved the unquestioned value of the even head position.

essential of uniformity and sound mechanics.

Before the youthful Morris, the foremost players swayed all over Scotland while they were swinging. They lunged at the ball and flogged it. Only by lucky timing, promoted by many hours of play, did a player manage to connect well with the ball. No wonder there were so few golfers competent enough to warrant national championships in golf's homeland, prior to the Morris, Jr. period. There were from eight to 17 British Open contestants each year from the competition's start in 1860 until young Morris won his last one in 1872.

In 1873 the British Open, played at St. Andrews for the first time away from Prestwick, drew a field of 26. Obviously pioneering Scots thought that they had found golf's "secret" even though Young Tom didn't write a book about the steady head. That 1873 Open, by the way, was won by Tom Kidd, a forefather of the Willie Kidds, father and son, who have been in the pro post at Interlachen in Minnesota's Twin Cities territory, for years.

The Swing = Player + Club. With a fairly steady axis of the swing having been established the next advance in golf's technology naturally would come in the spoke of the swing. This progress wasn't made quickly. For years the best of the golfers wheeled around onto the ball with a flat swing. Sargent thought that the hickory shaft and the design of wood and iron heads to get the hard molded gutta percha ball up off thinly grassed fairways and out of tough tangled rough and sand of Scotch links, probably favored retention of a swing that was primarily a matter of body turn and comparatively minor hand action.

Then along came Harry Vardon to turn attention to the manner of coupling player and club and manipulating the club so its face could be controlled with reasonable nearness to precision, thus the clubhead could be

SWAYING
Off line on the (forward) swing.

Harry Vardon emphasized sure-hand control via his famous overlap grip.

accelerated by the wrists smoothly into required speed as the ball was hit.

Vardon won six British Open championships; those of 1896, 1898, and 1899, with the hard "gutty" balls and with the American Haskell-type, cored, rubber-thread wound and molded-cover ball in 1903, 1911 and 1914. He won the U. S. Open in 1900 and finished second to Francis Ouimet in the play-off of our National Open at Country Club, Brookline, Mass., September 20, 1913, a day that lives in glory. All of a sudden the thin Ouimet kid became almost as distinguished as Boston's John L. Sullivan, an earlier and gaudier flower of American Sporting life.

From the time when Tom Morris won his last British Open championship until Vardon won his first, the quarter century must have been lively with golf experimentation of two types. The scholarly school was influenced by St. Andrews, a center of learning as early as the 12th century. St. Andrews' University (the oldest in Scotland) was founded in 1411. The Royal and Ancient Golf Club of St. Andrews which was founded in 1754 didn't get its "royal" tag until 1834.

The artisan school was the other branch of Scotch golf, with masons, carpenters and shoemakers starring. The two schools were pretty much integrated. The artisans had the gift of thinking with their hands, which isn't a bad deal in playing golf, and the collegians tried to figure out technique to beat the artisans, thus giving an early start to the fascinating confusion of golf theory.

Vardon was not a Scot. He was born on the isle of Jersey and went to work at 13 as a gardener for a Major Spofford who used to take Harry to play with him when other partners were not available. Vardon joined a workingmen's golf club on Jersey and won his first prize there. From Jersey he went to England to become professional at the Studley Royal Golf Club, a nine-hole course Lord Ripon had built on his estate near Harrogate. Vardon then was 20. The year was 1890.

GRIP
Full finger or baseball grip.

The old two-fisted grip already was being questioned. Several of the thoughtful amateurs of St. Andrews were using the overlapping grip that eventually was popularized by Vardon and often is identified by his name. The grip now is used by almost all better golfers. The most conspicuously successful exception is Jack Nicklaus. He uses an interlocking grip with the forefinger of the left hand and the little finger of the right hand curled around each other.

Vardon's dexterity, with the little finger of the right hand over the forefinger of the left hand, was phenomenal. He was especially skilled in maneuvering long brassie shots from those close lies of British courses to about 10 feet from the hole. George Sargent used to say there was foundation to the tale that Vardon, in playing an afternoon round on a course, would have to play some of his shots out of divots he'd made when he'd played his morning round.

Tommy Armour, as an amateur, played schooling rounds with Vardon. Vardon told Armour the reason for adopting the overlapping grip was that it kept the Vardon hands close together. Vardon held the club principally with his fingers instead of with the old-fashioned palm grip which had both thumbs around the shaft and the thumbs and first fingers showing two Vs over the center of the top of the shaft.

The Hands of an Artist. Vardon, by the way, was the first great golfer to have in his tactics controlled hooks and slices. That ability was valuable on the wind-swept British seaside courses.

There have been modifications of the grip that Vardon used. That was to be expected as Vardon had extra-ordinary hands, large with long and graceful fingers. There is a bronze of Vardon's hands on the grip of a golf club. Now and then you will see, in British golf clubhouses, that bronze casting molded from Harry Vardon in the life. Occasionally, you will see on grill-room walls of older American clubs photographs of Vardon when he and Ted Ray, winner of the 1912 British Open and 1920 U. S. Open, were on an American tour. There is one of those pictures at Longmeadow in suburban Springfield, Mass. The difference of the hands of a superb artist and the hands of the very good but not great golfers who also were in the group is conspicuous in that photograph.

In the Vardon era, as when Hagen, Jones, Armour, Sarazen, Hogan, Middlecoff, Snead and Palmer had to be beaten by whoever won a big tournament, the top golfer invariably handled his club with the finesse of a fiddling maestro using his bow.

Ben Hogan once wrote that delicacy of feeling is what is wanted in golf. In lectures by Jimmy Demaret, Frank Walsh, Tommy Armour, Horton Smith, Johnny Farrell, Joe Novak, the almost forgotten magical tutor, Eddie Loos, and several other notables, Esquire's pages have presented interpretations of the Vardon discovery of how to better handle a golf club.

There is no drastic variation from the Vardon grip as described by him in his "The Complete Golfer", published in 1905, and the adaptations Esquire's experts made to suit their individual conditions and which they recommended to readers.

Vardon's left hand grip had the shaft lying from the knuckle joint of the first finger across the ball of the second; perhaps slightly more in the fingers than the grip of some of the American moderns who have the shaft angling from the left forefinger knuckle a trifle more, so the club is anchored between the little finger and the heel of the left hand.

The Vardon idea of having the butt of the right hand thumb pressing hard against the thumb of the left continues to be standard operating practice with today's experts. Vardon said "The little finger of the right hand rides on the first finger of the left." Now most of the better golfers have the right little finger hooked around the forefinger of the left hand.

The Capricious Right Hand. The Esquire stars who wrote about the grip differed from Vardon when he wrote, "I grip quite as firmly with the right hand as with the other

16

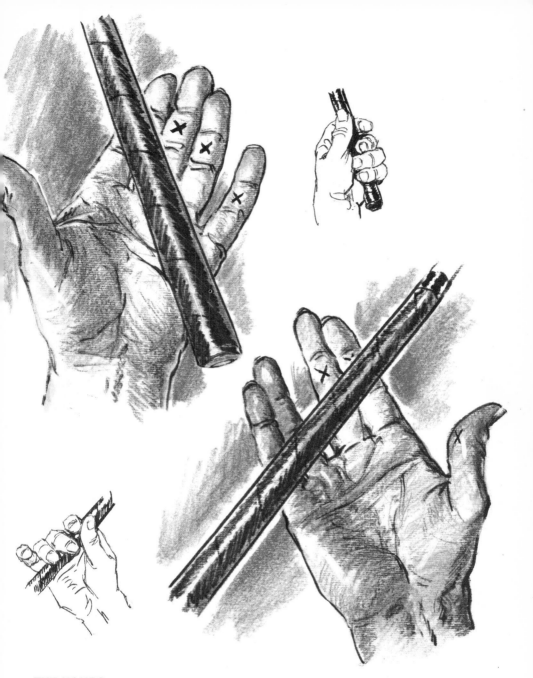

THE HANDS
In the left hand grip club rests on the middle joint of the index finger. There can be some slight variation in the placement of the butt end of the club. **The right hand grip** *must* remain with the fingers for sensitive feel and power control. **Not the palm.**

17

THE HANDS AND THE SWING
The pad of the right thumb must fold over and remain in contact with the left thumb throughout the entire swing. **Hold firmly with the last three fingers** of the left hand, and just firm enough to control the club with the first two fingers and the thumb of the right hand—mostly with the middle finger.

one. When the other way is adopted, the left hand being tight and the right hand simply watching it, there is an irresistible tendency for the latter to tighten up suddenly at some part of the upward or downward swing, and, as surely as there is a ball on the tee, when it does so there will be mischief. Depend upon it, the instinct of activity will prevent the right hand from going through with the swing in that indefinite state of looseness. Perhaps a yard from the ball in the upward swing, or a yard from it when coming down, there will be a convulsive grip of the right hand, which, with an immediate ack-nowledgement of guilt, will relax again. Such a happen-ing is usually fatal; it deserves to be. Slicing, pulling, sclaffing, and the foundering of the ball—all these dis-

18

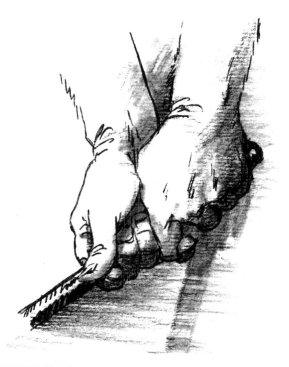

STARTING THE SWING
The hands *should not* **pick up the club** to start the backswing, except when a fast wrist break is intended. Normally, the swing should start with the left hand and left arm in control.

asters may at times be traced to this determination of the right hand not to be ignored but to have its part to play in the making of the drive. Therefore in all respects my right hand is a joint partner with the left.''

The American professionals writing in Esquire agreed with Vardon that "my right hand is a joint partner with the left," but they accented left hand strength in control of the club. Their thought was that, generally, the left hand was for control and the right hand for power and the combination had to be balanced by controlling the swing of the club in the desired groove until the time to apply power with the right hand.

There has been little argument with the Vardon statement: "Depend upon it, the instinct of activity will prevent the right hand from going through with the swing in that indefinite state of looseness." In their own play and in their teaching the American pros are strong with the left or right hands as required at stages of the swing. The primary reason for being stronger with the left hand than the right hand at address is to protect against the tendency to make the mistake of lifting with the right hand rather than correctly starting the swing with the left hand and arm in control.

The American professional favors slightly stronger grip with the left hand rather than agreeing with Vardon who wrote:

"The grip with the first finger and thumb of my right hand is exceedingly firm, and the pressure of the little finger on the knuckle of the left hand is very decided. In the same way it is the thumb and first finger of the left hand that have most of the gripping work to do."

Hogan, Armour, Palmer and the excellent instructor, Frank Walsh (who also was an able tournament player in the 30s), in their Esquire tuition are against thumb and forefinger emphasis in the grip. All of them stressed secure hold of the club by the last three fingers of the left hand hooked around the club grip and squeezing it with just enough force against the roots of the fingers to allow the wrist to cock freely at the top of the swing, but not so strong that muscles of the forearm are tightened.

They recommended that the first two or middle two fingers of the right hand be placed in position to whip right hand power into the shot. The right thumb and forefinger were placed pretty much in the function of feeling, rather than holding, elements.

In reviewing the way they adapted the Vardon grip you see that the moderns do not share the Englishman's fear of the right hand's "instinct of activity" bringing the hand into the shot at the wrong time, but considered this action as something to be used in the right place at the right time. The so-called "delayed hit" in which the right hand whips into the shot when both hands have been swung down about into the vertical plane of the ball, is a case of the Americans making confident and effective use of a right hand that had been merely riding along until it was needed.

The classic description of the coordination of hand work in the American version of the Vardon grip was made by Tommy Armour in his instruction articles. Tommy followed his Esquire treatises with a book in which he said in the chapter on *The Art of Hitting with the Hands,* "Hold the club firmly with the last three fingers of the left hand, let the left arm and hand act as a guide and whack the hell out of the ball with the right hand."

Some professionals remarked that Armour's admonition caused an epidemic of hooking and while it cured the chronic slicers it made many of their better golfers right-hand nutty. To the criticism Armour retorted that his urging to use the right hand vigorously shouldn't have misled anybody who could read as he also had instructed the golfer to hold the club firmly with the last three fingers of the left hand and let the left arm and hand guide the club.

STRAIGHT LEFT ARM

The Unbending Left Arm. Reference to the left arm as a guide tied in with the third major advance in modern golf technique that Sargent listed; the straight left arm as demonstrated by Bob Jones. In addition to the straight left arm's function as radius of the swing it also had leverage value, some authorities said.

Vardon's left arm was straight at address but at the

Bobby Jones' success reflected the asset of the straight left arm.

top of the backswing his elbow bent almost 90 degrees. The bent left elbow was common in the Vardon era and well into the Hagen time. Hagen's left arm wasn't bent as much as Vardon's. Possibly The Haig had been sensing the improvement that young Jones brought into golf form. The Jones left arm was so straight that it almost seemed stretched at the top of the backswing. Jones emphasized the importance of cocking the wrists fully at the top of the backswing. He kept the club beautifully under control with a finger grip that allowed plenty of flexibility without sacrificing security of the coupling.

Maybe there was something special about the Jones grip, but if there was he didn't recognize it because he was no one to hold golf "secrets" and would have made known any discovery that he thought would have helped other golfers.

Joe Novak, former president of the PGA did considerable research as head of the professional organization's Teaching committee. After an examination of 32 pros at the PGA 1943 championship he commented on how experts held the club so they could manipulate it subconsciously in getting the clubface into the desired position. Novak maintained that Jones and Lawson Little had the butt end of the grip held so gently it was almost "floating" at the top of the backswing.

Other stars, including all of today's experts, keep a close hold with the last three fingers of the left hand. Possibly an instinctive strengthening by Jones and Little of the left hand connection as they started swinging down quickly made their methods conform to the general pattern.

Vardon, Hagen and all other early and current experts of golf in this century had the left arm perfectly straight as the ball was struck. There were remarkable action photographs taken of golf swings when Sargent had stroboscopic movies made of golf's foremost quartette in the 30s; Miss Joyce Wethered, Jones, Hagen and Vardon.

George W. Beldam was the author and photographer of the informative book "Great Golfers—Their Methods at a Glance." The book was published in 1904. Some of its photographs were taken at about 1/1100th of a second and you will not see much clearer motion pictures of hitting the ball when you look at today's golf movies. There were action photographs of J. H. Taylor using a "driving mashie," which would be about a No. 4 iron today. There's not a great deal of difference in Taylor's style then and Venturi's style now. There aren't more than, maybe, a half dozen in the past 60 years of golf who have been Venturi's superior—or possibly, equal—as an iron player.

The Tight Right Elbow. In the years when American golf was establishing the world's golfing standard, diligent experimenting was blending into reliable form the fourth essential that Sargent noted, the close right elbow.

The older British professionals had been getting close to this discovery and Douglas Edgar, an English professional who migrated to the United States and eventually to the pro post at Druid Hills in Atlanta, wrote a book, "The Gateway to Golf," in which he made a case for the "inside-out" path as the basic swing of good golf. This called for swinging the club back inside the direction line then bringing it down so it never crossed the direction line until after the ball was hit.

The Edgar doctrine was interpreted by American golfers, with their baseball background, as swinging to hit to right field. It also was associated with the "left arm for steering, right hand for power" policy that was developing. Armour got the Edgar book and played educa-

Tommy Armour taught the lesson of keeping the right elbow close to the body.

THE PLANE OF THE SWING
The "inside-out" plane. The butt end of the club is pulled down, aiming at the ball. This contributes strongly to hitting power.

ROLE OF THE HANDS
Left arm for steering, right hand for power. The plane should be inside-out, as though hitting toward right field.

tional rounds with Edgar in learning that the "inside-out" swing called for keeping the right elbow down and close to the ribs.

This worked very well for Armour in allowing him to get his power into his shots without losing accuracy. Armour many times said that although he was called the Iron Master by golf writers he thought he was better with his woods in combining length with precision.

Hagen — around 1909-1912, as an assistant to Andy Christ, professional at the Country Club of Rochester (N.Y.), spent considerable time practicing. He was a hard worker. Something else you may not have known about the great Haig is that he didn't smoke and never had a drink until he was 26 and had won his first U. S. National Open. One of the younger Hagen's practice gimmicks was to put a handkerchief between his right arm and body, just under his right shoulder. That helped him to keep his right elbow down and close.

Ben Hogan has been a conspicuous exhibit of the value of keeping the right elbow in; and of nearly every other element of effective style. In words and deed Hogan made it clear that keeping the right elbow in and both elbows comfortably close together were positions necessary to a first class golf swing.

The American Way — hit, risk, work. Though George Sargent didn't mention revolutionary playing tactics as an American contribution to golf's progress, it was the dashing American style of play, hitting hard and taking a chance, that changed the game. Until Hagen came along and began winning, a shot into rough or a bunker often was considered irretrievably lost. Hagen made the recovery shot almost as much a part of golf as the drive, the fairway wood or iron and the putt.

PRACTICE

Intensive hours of work on the practice tee has been considered a characteristically American aspect of golfing improvement but long application to practice certainly wasn't an American innovation. The smart and stubborn Scots stayed at golf until they got it partially whipped—for the time being, anyway. Willie Park, Jr., practiced putting eight hours a day in the '80s and '90s and that probably beats any American time. The Scots worked hard at golf and many of them went at it intelligently and almost reverently. George Beldam's historic picture book of golf swings, which has been cited previously, was dedicated in March, 1904, to British Prime Minister, The Right Hon. A. J. Balfour "who has done so much for the Royal and Ancient game."

Harry Vardon wrote, "When Mr. Balfour first began to play he, under the guidance of Tom Dunn, actually spent a miserable fortnight in bunkers only, learning how to get out of them from every possible position. The right honorable gentleman must have saved himself hundreds of strokes as the result of that splendid experience, trying as it must have been, and he might be still better if parliamentary care did not weight so heavily on him."

So the modern golfer, amateur or playing professional, should not believe that he is a man who has been uniquely assiduous in trying to learn golf.

The way to learn golf is by playing, experimenting and practicing. Time after time the experts remind us playing mortals that the best they can do for us is to show what to learn. But the only way to learn to do it is to go to work and then make the shots.

GETTING
A
GRIP
ON
GOOD
GOLF

On one point every Esquire expert on technique is in agreement:

A good grip is the first essential of good golf.

A fellow can have a good looking swing but if there's a weakness in the coupling of player and club the swing will come apart before or when the club strikes the ball. If the swing is only average but the grip is good the hand, almost instinctively, will move the club into the ball well enough to offset some flaws in the player's method.

The sound of the club hitting the ball tells whether or not the player had a correct connection with the club. If you don't hear a smart solid smack when you connect with the ball your grip needs improvement. Something else also may be wrong about the way you're going at your shotmaking but the basic trouble is in the way you're holding the club if your shot doesn't sound like it has been made with authority.

Anyway, that's the opinion of great golfers who offer their versions of first aid to suffering friends.

Two stars who have the model grips of modern golf, Ben Hogan and Tommy Armour, talked about holding the club.

Hogan told, in March, 1943, about caddies who became great players not by mastering the mechanics of the game but by imitating a good player and becoming aware of the difference of feeling a good shot and the awkward feeling of a shot incorrectly made.

He added that most golfers don't recognize the sensation of a good swing hence are without a foundation of a game.

Armour was an excellent violinist in his youth; good enough to be a professional musician had he so desired. You can imagine what advantage in hand training that gave him over the great majority of golfers. He had very keen feeling of the club.

Feeling is difficult to describe and that may be why those who write about the technique of golf limit themselves to the mechanics plus general advice to hold the club about as gently as a knife and fork. Nearly all of them who refer specifically to the degree of tension of the grip say that the average golfer holds the club with

THE SOUND
The solid smack at impact tells a lot about the execution of the shot.

31

such strong pressure he locks himself out of a smooth, free swing.

The only one of the writers who doesn't go into detail about the grip in telling about the features of golf methods is Eddie Loos who says, practically, that as long as the player can feel that the swinging business is going to be done by and with the clubhead the grip is correct. This allows the individual plenty of leeway for discovery and coordination of the positions and pressures that best fit him.

Experimentation to learn exactly what minute adjustment is best for the player is a tremendously important part of schooling in good golf but it is only suggested (and then rather timidly) by the instructing and playing masters. The reason for being shy about this point is that the job of acquiring a satisfactory grip is something done wisely under the supervision of a patient teacher and by intelligent experimenting. Expert players have had so much trouble from slight and accidental changes in their own grips they'll seldom advise anything but the conventional over-lapping (Vardon) grip with the Vs of thumbs and forefingers pointing toward the tip of the right shoulder.

Yet a very small change in the angle at which the club lies across the roots of the left hand's fingers can make a tremendous difference in the security and flexibility of the grip. Holding the club too far towards the right hand finger tips can produce a grip that is as unreliably loose. Allowing the club to slip down too far into the palm of the right hand results in a grip that is too stiff and dead. That ruinous slip into the right palm will occur unless the thumb and forefinger are pretty close together in their lower sections.

Whether the left thumb should be "long" that is, stretched out on the shaft or "short" so the knuckle is humped a bit can be highly important in assuring control of the club. As a general rule the Esquire faculty recommends to the student body the long thumb to give adequate support and steadiness to the club at the top of the backswing.

And just where the left thumb should be on the circumference of the shaft is a subject of a few paragraphs. Some advise having the left thumb about directly on the top of the shaft at address particularly for the stronger and more adept golfers. Others emphasize that the left thumb at address should be a trifle to the right of center of the shaft.

That matter of thumb location, as minute as it might seem, may mean the difference between swinging the club with accuracy and confidence and swinging it only with hope.

Some tutors write that the right palm, if opened, should be squarely facing the target and the left palm be in an exactly parallel position. Other teachers approve having the right hand tilted a trifle to the right and the back of the left hand, correspondingly, slightly turned toward the sky.

If the ordinary golfer would try to go through the multitude of details about positions of elements in the grip he would get hopelessly confused, but attention to the little details of the grip is one of the many big differences between the common golfer and the extraordinarily good ones.

Until Hogan had made many experiments with his grip he was an erratic golfer. He duck-hooked drives until a man without his heart and determination would have cried like a baby. Then he found the perfect grip—the perfect one for Hogan, anyway. From that time on Hogan began playing with such consistent excellence that you could call him the greatest and not get much of an

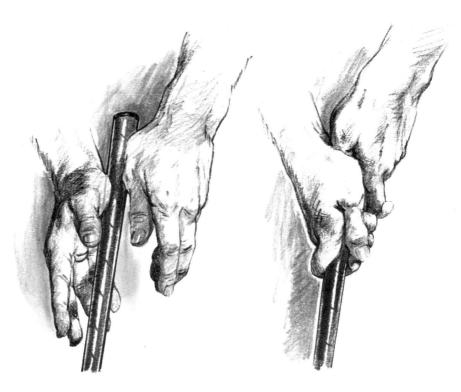

Both hands turn more to the left. Two knuckles will show on left hand; ball will tend to fade.

argument, even from those faithful to Jones, Hagen, Vardon, Palmer or Who Else?

Jimmy Demaret is reputed by authorities who know the methods of the sharpshooters to be a genius in his handwork with a golf club. Only Hagen is believed to have been Demaret's superior in delicately manipulating a golf club. Yet Jimmy didn't find out until just too late what was the perfect grip at the perfect time for him. Just before the 1957 National Open at Inverness Jimmy changed his grip a fraction of an inch and began swinging with power and precision that brought him to the finish one stroke back of the 282 at which were tied Dick Mayer and the eventual winner, Cary Middlecoff. Jimmy was 47 then. In 1961 he and Sam Snead won the

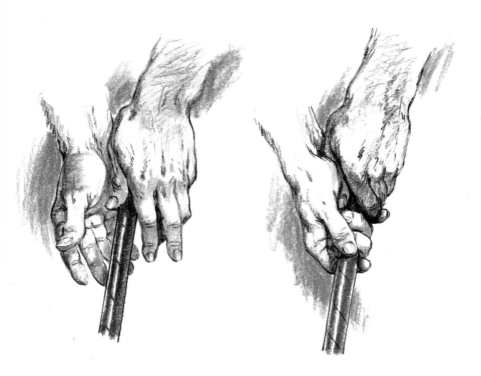

Both hands turn more to right. Three knuckles will show on left hand; ball will tend to hook.

Canada Cup at Dorado Beach, Puerto Rico. A great grip has kept Demaret a great player.

If you had read all the tutoring about the grip that professionals have written you would get the idea that the pros were trying to give directions that could be understood and applied to individual requirements.

All our experts agreed:

■ The major function of the left hand is control and that of the right hand is accelerating the clubhead at the correct time;

■ The left hand and arm are principal factors in swinging and the right hand and arm in hitting;

■ The left hand and arm in alignment swing the club back and away from the ball for if the right hand is in command in starting the backswing the club probably will be picked up too quickly and a sway to the right encouraged instead of the proper turning of the body;

■ The last three fingers of the left hand should be holding slightly stronger than the middle two of right hand;

■ The right hand fingers should be placed in position where they instinctively will strengthen when hitting begins;

■ Hands should be close together with the butt of the right thumb snugly over the left thumb;

■ The grip should be mainly with the fingers and the club never should be held in the palms of the hands.

Points where the savants don't get together are not many and, as has been mentioned, those differences may be more matters of individual requirements than of basic practice. For instance: a few endorse having the forefingers and thumbs of both hands as main holding elements, as old Harry Vardon recommended, but the majority of the moderns stress securing the club at all stages of the swing with the last three fingers of the left hand and using the middle two fingers as the power coupling of the right hand.

Joe Novak takes exception to the usual left hand rule. Novak maintains that the middle two fingers of the left hand do the holding well enough and if the little finger is hooked firmly around the grip there is created a slowing tension in the swing without any gain in control.

Tommy Armour recommends what he calls a trigger grip with the forefinger of the right hand hooked onto the shaft and the thumb a little to the left of the shaft. This sets up the grip for a lively lash with the right hand. Armour says that the largest third of the forefinger performs an important function in working on the shaft so it whips the club into the shot. He also reminds that the sensitive

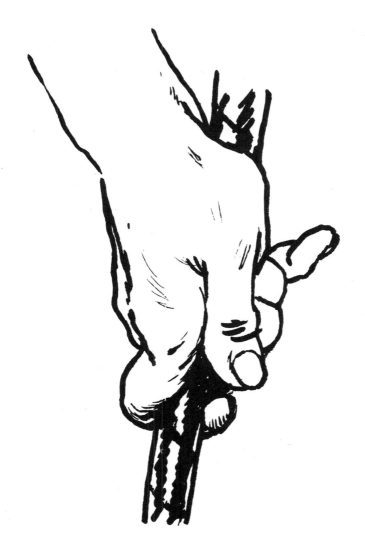

Trigger grip with the forefinger.

Interlocking – good for hands with short fingers.

touch of the tips of the forefinger and thumb provide feeling essential to a controlled strong shot.

There are references by Esquire's golfing authorities to the degree of pressures on tips and other places on fingers in holding the club with just the correct firmness and without promoting stiffening tension in the forearms. That is a matter the experts touch lightly as it seems to them to be something in which the right answers are to be learned by the individual through trial, error and triumph.

Only brief mentions are made of the interlocking grip and the ten-fingered grip. The interlocking grip with the left forefinger and the right little finger hooked around each other is OKed as giving some the highly desirable feeling of having the hands compactly together. The all-finger grip is approved as putting both hands on the grip so they work as a unit and as providing maximum "touch" of the club. The all-finger grip also is recom-

10 finger — good for small or weak hands.

mended as being logical for women with weak hands and for men with short fingers, although the experts often remind the student that the golf grip is not a connection in which strength must be great to keep the club under control during the swing and especially during contact with the ball. Flexible security rather than a tense and cramping clutch of the club is required.

Latitude in applying the details to the individuals is allowable but variations from the conventional must be made cautiously as enough error will creep into the grip without inviting it by departures from the time-tested normal methods of connecting player and club.

Features of the ideal grip may be summarized in specifying it as:

■ A connection that is, in effect, an extension of the arms;

■ A combination of control station and a power line;

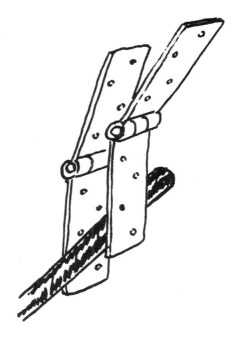

Using the wrists as hinges.

■ A firm, flexible joint;

■ A union that keeps the position of the clubface controlled fully yet does not develop tension that tightens the forearms and deadens the swing and hit;

■ A coupling that allows the wrists to hinge freely and properly so mainly centrifugal action will cock the club at the top of the backswing;

■ A coupling that develops and maintains sensitive feeling of the clubhead and, especially in putting, the "touch" that subconsciously determines the force needed for the putt;

■ A connection designed to have the hands function as a balanced unit;

■ A coupling that permits application of required clubhead speed at the right time;

■ A connection that will not allow the club to turn or jar loose at contact;

■ A union that has the hands staying together instead of separating at the top of the backswing;

■ A connection that minimizes tightening tension;

■ A connection that facilitates whipping the club into the shot;

■ A coupling that promotes hitting through the shot with the hands coordinated in a correct follow-through.

Without going into any anatomical detail the teaching about a grip to join the player and the club effectively often reminded the student that wrists are hinges, not power elements.

Occasional references to exercises for strengthening the grip pointed out that the idea was not to get the fingers and forearms in condition for bending steel bars, but for the capacity to maintain a firm coupling without tightening the forearms and shoulders with muscle strain. Finger pressure exercises on a piece of hose, or isometric exercises with fingers of both hands pulling against each other, were advised as measures that probably would be helpful to most golfers.

THE
STANCE
OR
THE
BEGINNING

You hit a golf ball when you are standing up, well balanced. If the average player could get a couple of pictures of the unposed way he usually stands to the ball a good teacher could show him why he doesn't look like a golfer and why he is lucky if he hits the ball.

One of those pictures would be made with the lens aimed squarely at the player and in a plane half way between the player's feet. The other picture would be with the lens on the direction line and facing the target. That's the spot Bob Macdonald, the pros' pro as a teacher, said was especially good for checking on a player's balance and the way that the clubface came against the ball. He remarked that you couldn't tell if a wheel was wavering by facing it as it whirled but you could if you were in line with its track.

The ordinary golfer is careless about his stance and posture as he addresses the ball. That observation, made years ago and often repeated by Esquire's golf teachers, continues to state the case.

In reviewing the instruction on addressing the ball there is only one change in the style made during about a quarter century and that is the manner in which the current stars bend their knees slightly more than their predecessors in making the shorter shots. Otherwise everything about the address is the same. It will be noticed that while the "sitting down" posture for the

WEIGHT AND FEET

Weight is evenly distributed on the feet, but a little heavier on their inner edges. For long wood shots the feet are spread about shoulder width. For shorter shots they move closer together. **For long shots** the ball is placed a little back of the left heel. **For middle irons** the ball is placed in the center of both feet. **On a teed up drive,** the hands are in line with, or a little behind, the ball so as to catch the ball slightly on the upswing. **For the irons** the hands are, and must stay, ahead of the ball to aid in hitting down, through and under the ball.

THE SHORT SHOTS
Weight is slightly back on the heels and the knees are slightly bent on shorter shots. The clubhead is coming into the ball from an inside-out plane. Stance is a bit open.

approaches is accented a bit the knees are not bent out in front. Stability is obvious as he addresses the ball for every shot. Although there seems to be a trifle too much weight on the heels that's much less dangerous to balance than weight being even a little bit forward.

There is complete agreement on the perfect foundation for the golf swing which has weight evenly carried between the balls of the feet and the heels and, at address, a little heavier on the inner edges of the feet.

THE FEET VS. THE BALL

One of the eternal verities of golf is that everything about technique is determined by the ball. Where the ball is and where you want it to go are the two and the only factors that rule every detail of making a shot.

The problem of playing the shot begins to develop as

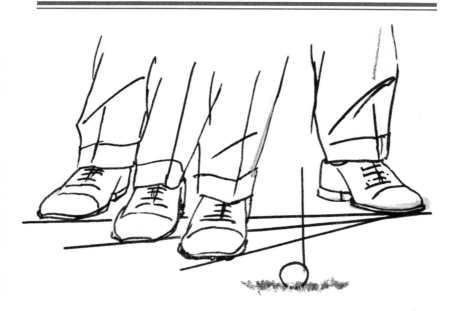

FEET AND STANCE
As the feet move closer together the stance opens. As a result, the backswing shortens. The ball may appear to have been moved back.

the player realizes he has to decide where to place his feet in relation to the ball. The correct answer is almost a matter of instinct to the experienced player but even he loses the combination of sight and feel and can't find just where to have the ball in addressing his shots. Particularly is he troubled when his timing isn't as it should be. Whether the fault is primarily in the tempo of his stroke or because of the location of the ball in the arc of his swing he doesn't know for sure. He will have to spend hours on the practice tee and costly rounds of play trying to regain satisfactory coordination.

Ben Hogan was quoted in Esquire:

"A great many golfers get up to the ball and don't even positively decide they are going to hit it. They change around, uncertain, then swing out of sheer, desperate confusion . . . I'd advise the average golfer, first of all, to know what he wants to do. Then be positive and not change his mind."

Being positive about the correct location of the feet depends on the:

Target;

Risks;

Lie;

Wind;

Plane of stance (up-hill, down-hill, side-hill, level);

Type of shot desired (trajectory, direction line);

Club to be used;

Type of swing.

The expert golfer places his feet so the bottom of the arc of his swing will come at the point the shot requires. If it's a teed-up drive the ball is to be caught on the up-swing of the driver which has a nearly vertical face; only tilted backwards about 10 to 12 degrees. Then the ball is played from a line about even with the back of the left

LOFT AND ARC
As the loft increases the arc becomes more upright. **At impact** the right knee bends in toward the ball, the hips move forward but the head and shoulders stay back. The wrists remain cocked until just before impact. They come into the ball "square" at impact and then roll over after impact.

heel; maybe an inch or so back but never ahead of that imaginary line.

THE HANDS VS. THE BALL

The hands, in addressing a drive, are about in line with the center of the body. In this location and with the ball approximately in line with the back of the left heel the club shaft must angle forward a bit in a sort of preview of its position in swinging up to hit the ball accurately.

Shots other than the teed-up drive are made by getting the leading edge of the club under the ball. In correctly using the more lofted clubs the leading edge gets under and ahead of the axis of the ball. That obviously calls for the hands being ahead of the ball at address; practically in the same plane as the bottom of the arc of the swing.

Often our experts reminded the readers that the club-head gets the ball up and on its way as the player hits down and allows the loft of the club to perform the function for which it is designed. This reminder never is widely heeded as the common fault of the ordinary golfer is to try to scoop the ball up.

As the loft of the club increases the swing is made

more upright by the experts as they play the ball nearer a line off the right toe. There is difference of opinion about whether or not the feet being closer together for the shorter shots takes care of having the feet correctly positioned in relation to the ball. If the ball is played from a line off the back of the left heel for the long shots, merely bringing the right foot closer to the left for the medium and shorter shots will adjust so the club will swing down and under the ball, comment some Esquire authorities. Others, while writing that the width of the stance generally is in relation to the length of the shot desired, advise that the player move a little bit to the left, in relation to the ball, as the desired length decreases.

MOVING WITH THE SHOT

Johnny Revolta, nominated by most of the great players of the past 30 years as the ranking genius of chipping and pitching, moves a trifle to the left as the distance of the shot lessens. He never was one to bang the ball long distances but within 50 yards of the hole he could shrink three shots into two by slapping approaches within a couple of feet of the hole.

Revolta has his right foot at a right angle to the flight line in his stance for the approach shots and opens his stance with his left foot as the shot needed is shorter. That's the way of most of the other stars from Jones to Palmer, although some open the stance a bit more than others until their bodies are about 45 degrees toward the hole.

TURNING THE TOES

You may watch at the practice tees of tournaments without realizing that you are viewing a great deal of experimenting in stance. The great players hit very few practice shots carelessly. One of the small but tremendously important details you might notice in practice and play of the experts is where the toe of the right foot is pointing at address. For the long and medium shots many of the stars have it pointed out a little. That seems to loosen them for a big, easy backswing. However, others go along with Hogan who says the right foot should be at a right angle to the direction line. The left toe invariably is turned out so there'll be nothing locked and the player can go through with the shot. The expert allows the swing to get finished. The ordinary golfer frequently gets himself in some position at address so he's compelled to put the brakes on his shot and not complete it satisfactorily.

Understanding and study of the stance are fundamentals of learning golf that the average golfer skips over lightly and quickly, hence never learns one of the two essentials of good golf that can be mastered standing still. The other essential, of course, is the grip.

HOW WIDE THE STANCE?

One point on which the authorities are unanimous in all of their references to the stance is that for the medium and long shots the inner edges of the shoes should be approximately as far apart as the tips of the shoulders. A bit wider stance for the big drive probably won't hurt but any excess in the width of the stance involves risk of stiffening the knees and shoulders, cramping the turn and risking the loss of stability. Whenever the instructors warn about the dangers of having the feet too far apart they add that a spread too wide is uncommon with the average golfer; he is more disposed to have his feet so close together he cannot turn fully and freely without falling out of balance.

THE STANCE AND THE HOOK OR SLICE

There are only a few references to the influence of the stance in producing a slice or hook. The open stance with

TO SLICE
Open — or slice stance.

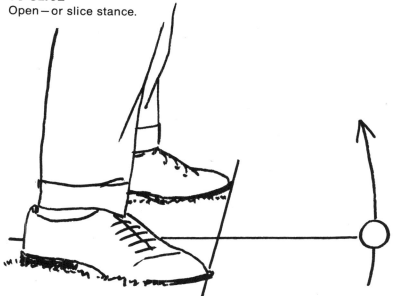

TO HOOK
Closed — or hook stance.

the right foot advanced a little and the left foot drawn back a trifle from the direction line is cited as favoring a slice by bringing the clubface from outside the direction line in and across the ball, spinning it clockwise. The closed stance with the right foot an inch or so farther back from the direction line makes it easier for the player to turn the body and swing the club from inside the line out across the ball so there'll be a counterclockwise hook spin produced.

HANDS, HOOKS, SLICES

None of the teachers wrote of hand position for deliberately hooking or slicing, seemingly believing that when the student was fortunate enough to get a good grip for hitting a straight shot he'd better not tamper with it when he could get the curved flight he wanted by adjusting his stance.

Repeatedly the writers pointed out that the reason for being so careful about stance and posture was that you must stand to the ball so your hands are enabled to get to the correct position at the right time.

Watching television golf, the student has to be warned against being misled by camera angles, particularly in looking at the position of the feet.

When the TV camera happens to give you a square view you will see that:

(1) Most of the experts have slightly closed stances for their drives; square stances for most of the rest of the shots except the short pitch and bunker shots for which they have open stances.

(2) The shorter the shot the closer the hands are to the body in the stance and in the execution of the shot.

As the player stands to the ball with a club that fits him the lie of the club and the length of the shaft (two elements which are coordinated in the properly designed

PRELIMINARY FOOT
POSITIONS

CLOSED

SQUARE

club) determine how far from the direction line the player's feet should be. The player should sole his club behind the ball so the foremost edge of the club is squarely across the direction line.

AIMING THE CLUB

One of the simplest little things that very few average golfers know is that the correct way to aim the club is to look from the target back to the ball, then adjust the leading edge of the club and after that adjust the feet and body and hands. The feet, hips and shoulders, also must be accurately aimed.

Aiming is only part of the job at address. Posture for balance which can be retained during the swinging hit is the other part. When you have the correct posture you do not have to reach for the ball, then when you begin to swing, your weight is transferred, if necessary, by turning rather than by leaning.

POSTURE AND BALANCE

In standing to the ball for the shorter shots the weight is mainly on the left foot and that accent does not change all through the shot-making. The experts are unanimous about that and underline their agreement by reminding that the short shots are almost altogether shoulder, arm and hand performances with only enough body turn to preclude stiffness and unsteadiness.

They all say the same thing in different words about the posture to attain and retain balance, providing a center of weight that virtually is the axis of the swing. They advise a slightly "sitting down" position with the knees bent and the behind pushed out a little. The chin is not close to the chest. The shoulders are loose.

What a lot of good golfers do to make sure that they have freedom for shoulder movement is to turn the head a little to the right at address. By that turn they give themselves more room for easily getting the left shoulder under the chin in the backswing. Back in the Jones era that slight turn of the head so the nose pointed a few inches to the right of the ball began to be used by leading

BALANCE IN SHORT SHOTS
Short shots are mainly a performance of the shoulders and hands. The body weight remains principally on the left foot throughout the swing.

players. It was considered a detail of address that helped them to keep their heads steady throughout the swing.

A SLIGHT CASE OF KNOCK KNEES

There is another feature of address that Hagen introduced and which now is pretty nearly standard operating practice with the headliners and that is what might be called the built-in forward press. All there is to it is to have the right knee bent slightly toward the left and the right foot slightly tilted so there is a little pushing sensa-

At address, right knee is bent toward the left.

tion on the inner edge of the right foot. The first movement in taking the club back begins transferring weight to the right foot and moving the hips around instead of to the right in a swaying action.

At address the arms hang down comfortably close to the body; never reaching out. The left arm is straight. Some of the good ones tell that they have a feeling the left arm is stretched but not to the degree of stiffening tension. The right elbow is bent a bit so it's fairly close to the body and about in line with the right knee. The left elbow points at the left hip.

Often the testifying stars tell of having the feeling that they are slightly knock-kneed as they address the ball. A few mention that they keep their elbows close together in somewhat of a "knock-elbowed" position without exaggerating the performance so there is a cramped feeling. They all say that the insides of the elbows at address should be toward the sky.

NOW: RELAX!

It is interesting to see how attention to relaxation grew in Esquire golf instruction articles. Almost anything said or written in this era of good golf about the mental or physical fundamentals of a fine game was said earlier by the studious Bob Jones. Others may have thought, said or written as Jones did for the great stars are brothers under the skull, but Jones always had the capacity to communicate clearly when he put his ideas down on paper, as for instance, when he wrote on Preparing for Competitive Golf:

"Golf is not exacting upon the physical powers of a man, but is trying upon his nerves, and the nervous strain usually reacts in some way upon the physical body."

Cary Middlecoff, writing on "The Winning Feeling,"

told about the mysterious muscle tone that "is everybody's secret of good golf. When the 105-shooter hits a fine shot—and he is going to make two or three of them a round—he has his version of the winning feeling when he stands up to those unusually good shots. And when every tournament player gets hot he has that same sort of feeling."

Dr. Middlecoff also commented:

"The winning feeling ... depends on many elements, of which I think posture is one of the most important in golf. My medical and dental training. taught me enough about anatomy to be conscious of the necessity of putting muscles into position so they can function in the right direction."

Middlecoff cited examples of posture that eased tension and allowed smooth, reliable operation of muscles. One example was when his friend and very competent instructor and player, Buck White, told him "pull your chin up." "Buck," said Doc, "saw I was dropping my head just a bit too much. I have a long neck and when I drop my head just the least bit more than I should the muscles tighten and my shoulder action is cramped."

The astute Middlecoff also noted that "synthetic golfers—the fellows who made themselves great, Nelson and Hogan, for instance—may have a slight advantage over the natural golfers because the synthetic golfers have to figure out the one correct position for their individual needs. The natural golfers simply trust to the positions to come naturally."

"Hogan ... finally got the winning feeling in everything from his toes to his finger tips ... The past few years he's lost his putting secret and I think it's because he has changed his putting posture the least little —but fatal—bit, and he can't find the old reliable position again."

And more from Middlecoff:

"There are times when I see slue-footed fellows standing practically pigeon-toed to the ball. They wonder why they don't even get past the first round in their club championships. They're licked before they begin to try to move the club."

HOW TO LOOSEN UP

The proper stage between stiffness almost to rigidity and relaxation without limpness, is an essential of address that the experts talk about but can't describe. Each golfer has to find the ideal tone of muscles for himself. Maybe it will come while taking the advice of Al Ciuci, a veteran professional thoroughly seasoned, for he started Sarazen to greatness and Sarazen himself now is in advanced stages of a lively veteran's career. Ciuci, in an article on using the wedge to get out of trouble, remarks that the golfer wouldn't get into much trouble if he would "Try to loosen up a few minutes on the practice tee before playing."

"Loosen up," is the earlier term for what became "relaxation" in golf instruction gospel. Another development in the game's semantics now is being seen. What invariably used to be referred to as "concentration" is often called "carefulness" today. "Concentration" may imply an intensity that creates tension while "carefulness" might be a definition of good organizing, without strain or distraction, for the desired performance.

Tommy Armour had to teach himself how and how much to relax. He did an enviably successful job. Possibly no other one of golf's great artists has had Armour's understanding of the temperament and technique (if any) of the common golfer. Armour now plays as a club member and teaches budding young men and women champions as pilgrims to the master, not as paying pupils. For more fun and research he plays with other club members, in New York in the summer and Florida in the winter.

In an Esquire article on "How to Beat Your Slump," the Silver Scot said:

"From my own experience and observation, I've found that the hardest thing about curing a slump is learning to take it easy."

"Taking it easy" isn't learned easily. The golfer generally is the type Ben Hogan referred to in an article in Esquire on "Learning Golf by Sense," when he wrote:

"When pros talk together about their instruction problems, almost invariably they refer to the first and most important step in teaching as that of getting the pupil to relax.

"Why is this relaxation so vital? It has a lot to do with the basic principle of the method I'll give you for learning good golf.

"Why do you grit your teeth, hunch your shoulders, get tense and taut when you expect pain? The reason is that you thus hope to deaden your sensibility to the feeling of pain. When you are relaxed you believe that you'll feel too acutely. Delicacy of feeling is what we want in golf; hence the high value pros place on relaxation."

Nobody's been able to beat that analysis of the importance of establishing the correct muscle tone for the whole performance as one addresses the ball to make a shot.

The realistic Armour has some more to say about the golfer who can't get loose from himself:

"Watch at the first tee of any course and see drives pushed to the right or that are smothered, aborted hooks. The players are almost frozen. They can't get themselves unlocked so they can stand up easily, swing without

hurrying and hit with their hands. They get scared of nothing and instead of a swing have a spasm."

There you have the post-mortem that accounts for a lot of first tee "mulligans."

Inability to attain the correct balance between tension and relaxation is a problem the golfer has to solve for himself. There doesn't seem to be a thing the experts can do for him except to tell him what he's up against.

THE CHAIN REACTION OF TENSION

The problem may be broken into sections as Armour did in warning against locking the knees or against holding the club tight. He said there's a chain reaction from the tight grip that stiffens the forearms, then the shoulders are tightened, then the neck, back and hips get rigid and eventually the brain gets stiff. When the brain gets stiff a decent shot simply couldn't be made, Armour concluded.

The baseball player, as he stands at the plate and feels awkward halts the game, steps out of the batter's box, relaxes and begins all over. The golfer when he stands by his shot and feels tight and uneasy, rarely walks away and gives himself another chance to get into mental and physical equilibrium. Why? If you can give yourself the right answer to that question and can apply it you'll be better than 95 per cent of your fellow golfers.

THE
ANATOMY
OF
THE
GOOD
SWING

You've got to play golf to really learn it.

Anyone with normal athletic aptitude who plays golf four or five times a week can't hardly help being good. If he could putt worth a damn he would be much better (so he will admit).

But the ordinary golfer who has to make his living at something other than golf rarely gets enough time at the game to develop a reliable, keen feel for fine shot-making. No wonder he is looking for a "secret" that will give him the right answer quick and easy. Nevertheless golf is a game and shouldn't be as disturbing as he sometimes makes it.

The typical member of a first class private country club in north central and northeastern states plays between 35 and 50 rounds a year and those rounds are, usually, at varying intervals. He will play two or three days in succession during the summer then may not have a club in his hands for two weeks.

Handicap records at numerous clubs show a relationship between the amount of golf played and the players' scores; the more golf, the lower the player's score. Of course when a fellow's playing well he wants to play more often but the private club member generally has business responsibilities that restrain him from getting over-golfed.

The primary demands of making a living also keep the country club member from spending much time in trial-and-error learning on the practice tee. He cannot acquire good golfing habits as the playing professional has done; constantly repeating correct procedure in practice so it becomes second nature in play. The typical businessman golfer has to do his practicing as he plays. Not many of his type get a game well enough organized to do anything definitely but merely walk up, get hazily bewildered about some detail, then swing before getting mentally and physically into the clear.

The golf swing is a blend of details, balanced and in orderly arrangement by instinct more often than by deliberation. Knowledge of the details eliminates, not creates, confusion when this know-how is applied in fitting the details into a dependable composite. Esquire's golf experts have tried persistently to put across the idea of organized procedure as the one thing sure to help the average golfer.

Unanimously the experts agree that any golfer who attempts to apply, consciously, any more than one detail of what he knows about the swing during the fraction of a second required for a swing, is not in his right mind—or won't be for long. But, you've always got to think about one thing you must do at the right time, plus what the earlier British golf scholars called the "categorical imperative" when hitting the ball.

That job of hitting the ball is divided into three parts: the grip, the address and the swing.

Then the swing is divided into three parts: balance, position and timing.

Two of the three factors involved in hitting the ball can be correctly cared for while the player is standing at the ball. If he makes any appreciable errors in his address or grip in these preparatory, static departments of his technique, he will have to depend on luck or instinct to swing successfully.

The dynamic part of golf is a swinging hit. This stroke is good only when the head is held fairly steady, but not stiff-necked, to establish a fixed center of the swing and when the hands provide a connection between player and club that enables the player to control the position of the face of the club and the timing of the blow.

There hasn't been any consequential change in the methods of the earlier or later Esquire golf writers who have starred as players. Certainly as far as the golfer who plays for fun is concerned, there isn't any difference between the technique of Jones, Hagen, Armour, Nelson, Hogan, Snead, Demaret, Little, Boros, Littler, Palmer, Nicklaus, Casper, Venturi, Lema, Nichols and Player. A golfer today who is able to imitate reasonably well the Jones methods of 35 years ago and who can putt like any of today's first ten money-winners on the tournament circuit would be among today's brightest stars. Hogan, who stands about halfway between the Hagen and the Palmer periods, showed in the 1964 Masters and PGA tournaments that, had his putting been equal to that of the winners of those events, he would have given them tough competition for first place.

Jones once said that he couldn't see any fundamental differences in the swings of his era and of the present. Now the stars' backswings aren't as long and as leisurely and a bit slower. Perhaps a stiffer manner of "sighting" the shot also is a difference between the periods, according to Jones. Jones said that in the 1920's he discovered that he could get to an effective position at the top of the swing from normal address position by swinging the club directly over the right shoulder, assuring a full cocking of the wrists, while fully rotating his trunk to the right as he kept his head immovable and used his spine as an axis. Then he lifted his hands and arms straight up to the normal top of swing position.

From understanding to action in improving golf is a vast gap to span for the simple reason that the intelligent golfer rarely has enough time to spend in getting the feeling of what movements are right, then to make those movements matters of habit.

You read about W. C. Fields practicing four or five hours every day for five years on a juggling routine before he put it into his act. The famed clown Grock practices 14 or 15 hours a day on a detail of his show. There is a beautiful blonde Danish young woman known as the "Ballerina of the Bicycle." Perhaps you have seen her on television programs. She practiced 13 hours a day for seven years in perfecting her performance. Paul Hahn, the trick shot golfer, estimates that he has spent at least 5,000 hours practicing some shots in his repertoire. Even though the game of the much-better-than-average golfer allows a wide margin of error he cannot wish himself into a satisfactory method but has to think and do some work in attaining a style of swinging that will send the ball where he wants it to go.

In many details the swing of golfers varies as their handwriting would vary. Each fellow has to swing the club back and up and down and through according to his own physique and temperament and that gives him a rather elastic pattern.

The great golf teachers realize that the golf club member isn't going to be able to closely imitate the proficient golfing specialist, hence instruction must be provided in a way that will encourage practical interpretation and adaptation.

FITTING CLUBS TO THE BODY

Teaching professionals comment that what many golf-

66

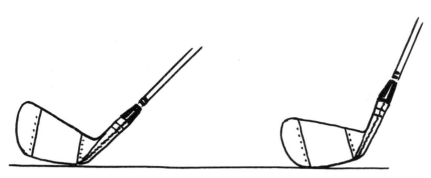

FITTING THE CLUBS
Clubs that do this are poorly fitted to you.

ers need is better fitting clubs rather than more instruction. They see a player stand to the ball with the toe of the club up or down instead of the sole of the club being flat on the ground back of the ball, and with the hands reaching out for the ball instead of hanging down comfortably close to the body. With such handicaps of badly fitted clubs how can the golfer do as Bob Jones advises and easily swing the club over the right shoulder?

THE PLANE OF THE SWING

When you've got clubs that fit you the plane of the swing—meaning the angle from the imaginary vertical axis of your body—will be correctly adjusted to your build. If you are of average build the plane of the swing will be about 45 degrees. If you are a bit on the chunky side, you will find that a flatter swing will be more natural. If you are thinner and taller than the average you instinctively will swing in a more upright plane.

Some experts referred to two planes of the swing with the correct downswing being a trifle flatter than the upswing. That sort of a change of angle resulting from a loop at the top of the backswing was regarded as good form but if the loop at the top threw the clubhead out-

With the player of average build the plane of the swing with the woods will be about 45°. As the clubs shorten the plane becomes more upright to 70° or 72°. The short build player will use a flatter plane.

side the plane of the backswing you were out of luck.

As one studies the textbook material, he discovers that all the good teachers are saying practically the same thing: never allow your hands to get farther from your body than their position at correct address. That position establishes the plane of the swing. They also stress that you must keep your right elbow pointing downward as you swing back. Then your downswing, the first movement — getting your left side set as the axis — will bring your right elbow quite close, but not cramped, against your ribs.

THE VERY CRUCIAL BACKSWING

The authorities repeatedly say that if your backswing is correct your chances are very good that the hitting part of your swing will be as it should be.

On how to start the backswing experts are not altogether in agreement. Some great players believe in the forward press. Others do not. There also is difference of opinion about how the forward press should be made; whether it is simply an unlocking movement with the shoulders and hands moving slightly to the left or soleing the club behind the ball then moving the right knee to the left and letting the "rebound" start the backswing without a jerk. Jones wrote that after placing the left foot into position then moving the right foot into place, the club is grounded behind the ball. Then comes a little waggle of the club. After that there is a slight forward twist of the hips that breaks the tension then the rebound starts the swing. Jones pointed out that the hands have nothing to do with his version of the forward press; the movement is in the legs. By setting the hip turn in motion a smooth start of the swing is assured and the inclination to pick up the club with the hands and the arms is mastered, said Jones.

Cary Middlecoff made an interesting comment on the forward press when he said that perhaps the reason he didn't feel the confidence he should have in trap shots was because the rules didn't allow him to ground the club behind the ball and start his swing with a forward press. It may be significant that few ordinary golfers start with a forward press but stand at the ball and begin the swing by nervously yanking the club away.

In reviewing references to Hagen's technique mention was made of The Haig's "built-in" forward press at address with the right knee bent a bit to the left and the left hip turned a little more than the right shoulder toward the hole.

There are pictures of Hogan, showing him with a belt around his knees, a practice gimmick that, in effect, had his right knee turned toward the left and weight decidedly on his left foot at address. The first movement in the backswing then would require turning rather than swaying, hence Ben was suggesting a method of avoiding the first and fatal error in the swings of most ordinary golfers; the mistake of swaying laterally to the right.

A backswing is a swing to the back. That means you've got to swing the club around and to the back and get into the backswing enough of a windup to get yourself coiled for a swinging down into the ball.

The initial stage of the backswing advocates the "one-piece" start, according to most authorities. The one-piece start is simply a turning of the left side with the left arm and the shaft in line. It is a swing away from the ball. The main change in the "one-piece" start in years has been that the younger stars keep the left foot nearly flat on the ground during the backswing. They do what Alex Morrison once advised; roll onto the inside of the left foot. Morrison added that after rolling onto the inside of the left foot, the heel should come off the ground a little.

THE ROLL OF THE WRISTS

A few of the tutors advise cocking the wrists slightly at the beginning of the backswing of every shot. Nearly all the very good ones tell you to play a wedge shot out of sand by quickly cocking your wrists after you begin your backswing but not many advise this procedure on

STARTING THE SWING

The initial stage of the "one-piece" swing gets you turning away from the ball. It starts by the turning of the left side with the left arm and the shaft in line. The left foot rolls onto its inner edge, the heel leaving the ground very little.

every shot. Most of the authorities counsel swinging the club back and around and up with the straight left arm swinging from the left shoulder. They warn you not to have your wrists hinge until that bending is caused by the right elbow staying down and close to the player and, further, by centrifugal force near the top of the back-swing.

In general, the straight left arm swings the club back and forward to the place where the right forearm and hand do the hitting. Then there comes that stage of the stroke when the right arm becomes as straight in hitting through the ball as the straight left arm is in the back-swing and in swinging the club down to the ball.

Tommy Armour remarked some years ago that every good golfer keeps his head steady, hits down at the ball and hits with the hands. That appraisal still holds good.

POSITIONING THE HEAD

Holding the head steady but without tension in the shoulders during the swing is just as essential to good golf today as it was in the 1860's when young Tom Morris discovered that when he kept his head rather still he played well and when his head moved noticeably his opponents were hard to beat. When the aspiring golfer learns that old stuff the fancy details aren't too hard to master.

There isn't anything new about visualizing the head as the hub of the swing. Arnold Palmer has his head still so part of his left shoulder goes under his chin at the top of a full backswing and his head doesn't move appreciably until after his right shoulder goes under his chin as the club is whipped through after the ball. Tom Morris, Jr., Harry Vardon, Francis Ouimet, Walter Hagen, Bob Jones and all the other stars were steady-headed golfers. There's no other way to getting an effect-

72

ive, consistent swing. There were many Scotch professional builders of American golf who taught their pupils good sound swings with the shoulder-chin advice as the first fundamental of swinging technique.

The American kids who acquired their golf styles as imitative caddies were quick to see that the head had to stay nearly still without restricting shoulder action.

In 1911 Johnny McDermott became the first American-born professional to win the USGA National Open. He'd been introduced to golf as a caddie in Philadelphia. At Chicago Golf Club where he won the first of his two National Open Championships he defeated in a play-off Mike Brady who'd started in golf as a caddie at Boston, and George Simpson, a Scot, then the professional at the Wheaton, Ill. Golf Club. Brady lost another play-off for the National Open Championship in 1919 when Hagen beat him by a stroke.

Brady has been a durable exhibit of good form for many years in the PGA Senior championships. He says that the first thing the early American caddies learned about golf was that a golfer had to stay perfectly balanced during the swing and to stay in balance you had to keep your head steady, whether you were hitting with all your might or trying to hole an 18 inch putt.

Johnny Revolta is one of the busiest of the decidedly successful golf teachers today. In one of his Esquire texts, "Don't Become a Deadhead," he related:

"Almost without exception I find that golfers whose progress in playing has come to a stop are not suffering from 'looking up' but from inability to look up properly and have the eyes catch up with the flight of the ball when it's 40 or 50 yards off the clubhead. Unless they allow their eyes to follow the ball they freeze the swing ... Your head should rotate slightly with the movement

*of the shoulders . . . any motion that tends to restrict
freedom of action in golf is potentially dangerous . . .
In the backswing many keep their eyes so glued on the
ball that their heads tilt toward their left shoulders. This
completely destroys balance."*

KEEPING THE NECK UNFROZEN

Reference has been made to the Jones mannerism of
pointing his nose slightly to the right of the ball at address. Revolta, in urging the reader not to freeze his
neck as he makes his shot, also cites the Jones example:

*"Jones made a discovery, which I suspect he didn't
analyze correctly, when he adopted the habit at address
of turning his head slightly toward the right. Jack West-
land (National Amateur champion in 1952) adopted
that habit. The general interpretation was that the action
of cocking the left eye at the ball enabled Jones to keep
his head still. What happened (as close examination
of motion pictures discloses) is that the action permitted
Jones to rotate his head properly and get perfect timing
instead of being distracted by all he'd heard and absorbed consciously or subconsciously about keeping his
head still."*

Revolta, while not suggesting that the head bob, nod
or rock noticeably, tells the golfer not to worry about
head steadiness to a degree that cramps action. He notes:

*"When the typical golfer stands to the ball invariably
he is too tight — almost locked — partially because of
the psychological situation that confronts him and partially because he is intent on details that are certain
to lock him."*

Revolta makes it plain that over-accenting the steady
head is one of the ruinous locking details.

So, again, the easy medium is the right answer in golf
form.

CONTROLLING THE HEAD
The head should rotate with the movement of the shoulder following impact of the ball. Restricting this action tightens the entire right side and prevents smooth follow-through. The head generally moves down slightly on the backswing. **At impact** the head may swing slightly toward the right shoulder as a natural move to keep the upper body weight behind the ball.

Whatever slight movement of the head that is allowable in a perfect stroke is a trifle up and down movement on the vertical center of weight or the least little bit away from the ball—never with the shot—as the ball is hit. The unlocked knees and shifting of weight may cause a very small fall and rise of the head during the swing. Possibly determination to keep the head "back of the ball" accounts for movement of the head away from the ball that is discernible in action photographs Esquire presented.

If the player will keep his knees unlocked and "sits down" a trifle to the ball at address so he can swing freely, he won't have to give any attention to whether or not his head rises or falls a little during the swing. Keeping his head from moving ahead of the ball is very important. Maybe he can overcome that tendency by deliberately rolling his head to the right as he hits in the fashion the experts have as pretty nearly standard operating practice. This is something for the average golfer to determine by intelligent experimentation and practice.

WORKING WITH THE FEET

As groundwork of a stable swing, foot action shows some change during the years of the Esquire school. All the earlier stars were freer with the left foot than today's experts. However, none of the luminaries of the Vardon, Hagen, Jones, Nelson, Hogan and Snead heydays let the left heel get very far off the ground during the backswing for medium or full shots. They kept weight principally on the left foot in making the short shots that didn't call for much body turn.

The older style of left foot action generally was a turn as well as a lift of the heel, almost as though an imaginary spike went through the ball of the big toe. Look at the pictures of swings by Vic Ghezzi, Jimmy Thomson,

Horton Smith, "Jug" McSpaden, Lawson Little, "Buck" White, Toney Penna, Bob Hamilton and Jack Burke, Jr. and you see, especially in Burke's case Jack rolling onto the inner edge of his left foot rather than lifting his left heel and swiveling on the ball of his big toe in making a big backswing.

Burke was regarded as the paragon of the young school. Hogan and Snead settled themselves solidly on the right foot in winding up for a big shot and made no effort to keep the left foot on the ground and cramp their swings. They have lasted long at the top of the parade, so maybe there is something to the observation of older teachers and players to the effect that if you twist too much with your left foot nearly anchored you're going to have back trouble and a lot of it.

ACTION OF THE KNEES

Examining the aforementioned photographs and any of the motion picture frames of today's action films, you note what Tommy Armour says is a significant element of a swing: knee action.

Armour insists that the left knee has got to turn to the right until it points back of the ball on the medium and long shots, also the right knee never must stiffen and get stuck but must come into the shot if there is to be correct body action. With the right knee coming into the shot the body is brought parallel to the direction line as the power shots are hit. The body turns to face the hole as the swing carries itself to completion. In making the short shots that are mainly a performance of the shoulders and hands the left knee can dip a trifle toward the ball but not when there is much of a body turn required, says Armour.

There is the reminder, in the lesson literature, that the shoulders can turn without the hips or knees turn-

PEAK OF THE BACKSWING

At top of the backswing, the right leg feels well braced but not stiff. **The hips** have been turned by the left knee turning in toward the right. **The foot** has rolled onto its inner edge. **The heel** is off the ground a bit. **The head** is held still so part of the left shoulder goes under the chin. **The club shaft** does not go below the horizontal.

ing. Thus, the fellow who thinks he is cranking up for a powerful shot actually may be only turning his shoulders and not his body or setting his legs for the big smooth shot.

HANDS DURING BACKSWING

One of the points on which the instructors agree is that there should be no rolling of the wrists in the backswing. The club is to be swung by the extended left arm with the last three fingers of the left hand maintaining a firm, flexible connection so the wrists cock spontaneously at the top of the swing. The orthodox position at the top of the swing has the hands close together so the right hand, if opened would be in what is called the "waiter's position," meaning that a tray could be carried on the palm of the hand. That position is a natural result of keeping the right elbow down and close to the body while the left arm swings straight, but not rigidly.

BRACING FOR THE DOWNSWING

Another check point at the top of a full swing is the right leg being inclined toward the target. The knee never gets locked. The shoulders are almost square to the target. Most of the stars say they feel that they are well braced on the right leg at the top of the full swing but they can't tell whether that feeling is the result of a transfer of weight to bear heavier on the right foot or whether it is the sensation one is bound to experience with the right side acting as the axis of the backswing.

At any rate, there is a feeling of being confidently poised and looking at the ball over the left shoulder when the student has been able to get to the top of the backswing in pretty much the manner of the star.

THE PAUSE IN THE SWING

At the top of the swing the better players almost invariably pause perceptibly although several of them declare they are not aware of this very brief hesitation and doubt that any pause is advisable because of the risk of the rhythm being broken by the tiniest halt. Motion pictures of nearly all the experts show the club sharply defined at the point farthest back of the backswing, thus indicating that even with a little loop in changing direction of the club there is a halt for a fraction of an instant.

Regardless of what any playing expert may have against the hesitation at the back of the swing successful instructors usually recommend it to their pupils. The teachers remark that the pause encourages the ordinary player to steady himself so he can start down by getting his left side set firmly as the axis of the downswing. Furthermore, the pause minimizes the tendency to incorrectly start the downswing with a flip of the clubhead which is a common error of the average golfer. This premature uncocking of the wrists throws away the chance of correctly whipping the club swiftly through the ball.

THE RHYTHM IN THE DOWNSWING

The experts are 100 per cent for firming the left side in initiating the downswing. Some advise sliding the hips toward the target as the starter. Others say that simply setting the left foot firmly on the ground will be no restriction of body action. Armour says that advice is superfluous and confusing as all the player has to do is to get his right knee going into the shot and the left side will move correctly.

Pulling the left arm down so the butt of the club points toward the ball is one of the "musts." As the straight left arm has established the radius of the swing it is doing the steering into the position where the right forearm and hands start hitting. The pulling and the body turning bring the right elbow close against the ribs.

When the body and arms move the hands until they are about in the same vertical plane as the ball, the wrists being to uncock. Up to that stage the left arm and the shaft of the club are practically in a right angle arrangement. Then is when the oft-mentioned "late hit" begins.

There may be a lot of minor variations in the styles of all the good ones up to the hitting point then the personalities vanish and the ball doesn't know who's hitting it. At that point there is only one correct way.

STEER WITH THE LEFT, SMASH WITH THE RIGHT

The left arm and hand continue to do the steering but it is the right side that hits. And it strikes like lightning for it is the speed of the clubhead that accounts for distance.

Look at the right forearms of Jack Nicklaus, the slender Chi Chi Rodriguez, big George Bayer, Arnold Palmer, Tony Lema, Bill Casper or any other of today's long hitters and you will see what they have in common with Lawson Little, Jimmy Thomson, et al, who were mighty hitters. They all have right forearms of the spring steel sort. When they get the left arm and the right elbow positioned to have the right arm straighten at the right instant the ball is going to be flattened then rebound with a getaway like a shot.

At the moment of truth, when the club is hitting the ball, the stars want the head to be steady as the fulcrum of the efficient swing. Billy Casper says that the principal thing he thinks about when he hits a shot—a power shot or a putt—is to keep the back of his left hand moving squarely toward the target. When that happens the right arm straightens and the two hands, working in unison, throw the club after the ball.

There is no restraint—no braking—to the follow-through of the power shots of the big hitters. They finish

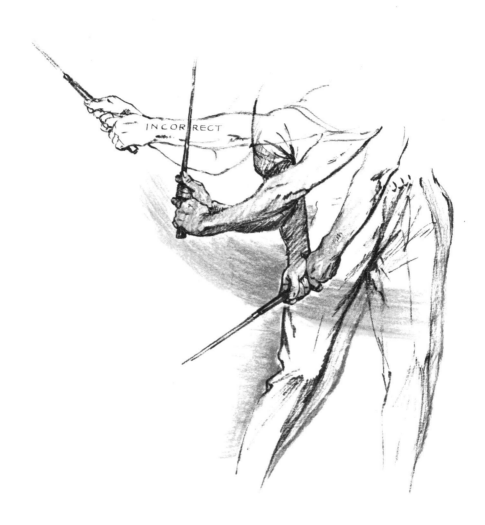

THE COMPLETE SWING
Premature "uncocking" of the wrists throws away the chance to correctly whip the club swiftly through the ball. **The right knee** goes into the shot. **Pull the left arm down** so the butt of the club points toward the ball. **The right arm** straightens and the wrists uncock correctly permitting the "late hit", which accounts for great clubhead speed.

THE FOLLOW-THROUGH
There is no restraint—no breaking—to the follow-through of power shots. Finish with hands high and the belt buckle facing the target.

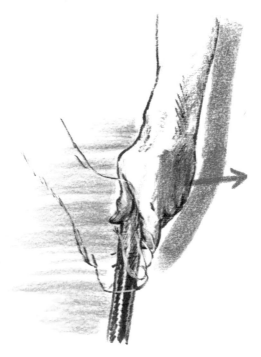

THE HIT
At impact the back of the left hand is moving squarely toward the target. The high point of the wrists is leading the hand. No restraints—no breaking—to the follow-through of the power shot. Finish with the hands high and the belt buckle facing the target.

with their hands high and with the strong boys facing the target.

The ordinary golfer flinches as he connects with the ball because he is losing control of the club, due to a faulty grip, or falling out of balance because of error in his stance and posture or because of a jerky swing. When the average player does go through with the shot, he frequently swings around with his shoulders almost horizontal, instead of completing his swing in a place that's about 45 degrees from upright so he can bring the club effectively into the ball.

GIVING SWING ENOUGH TIME TO HAPPEN

An essential of the good game is good timing and it's the most difficult feature to write about in a way to help the reader.

All that has been written about timing in producing a satisfactory shot is wrapped up by a veteran professional, Cy Foster. Foster is representative of hundreds of experienced pros who, at club lesson tees and at ranges, have made pretty fair golfers out of unpromising prospects. These men have to make their lessons simple and sharp to penetrate the bone and muscle curtains of their clients.

Foster says that good timing in golf means giving a swing enough time to happen.

That definition explains considerable of the average player's trouble.

In reviewing the gospel of golf as set forth by the game's greats, you see the chronology of the expert's swing. Then with only the qualifications of a locker room pro you can compare accurately the model with the timing of the common golfer. The expert takes time to study the situation. He deliberately or by habit considers the shot required, the lie, the wind, the club to do the business and his confidence in its use, the golf architectural factors and his competitive status at the moment. He aims carefully. He saves time by taking his time to get soundly organized.

The ordinary golfer walks up to the shot, quickly takes out a club, wriggles his feet around and spasmodically snatches the club away from the ball then begins throwing himself at the ball before what he calls a backswing is completed.

Timing, tempo, rhythm, smoothness — all those terms that involve coordination — are in the swing only when the swing is unhurried.

Proper pace of a swing is set by temperament. The ordinary golfer is confused by hearing that a fast backswing is ruinous yet sees stars swing back swiftly then hit the ball perfectly. A slow backswing for these proficient and fast-moving fellows would be awkward.

An interesting thing about timing may be witnessed in tournament play. The star who is performing at his normal rate on the tees and fairways will get on the greens and slow down to an unnatural degree then wonder why his putting isn't up to the standard of the rest of his game. This exhibition of costly variation in tempo is especially apparent to the golf student who watches tourney golf on television. When the stars have hot putters they are putting without the irksomeness that allows the viewer to go out in the kitchen and get himself a couple of snorts while an expert is preparing to try to make a simple putt. The delay throws even the best of them out of timing.

THE EXPERTS POINT OUT

Often bad timing is the effect of a flaw in balance or grip. When the backswing is begun with a jerk or a quick lift of the club by the right hand the experts point out that the errors probably are caused by (1) lack of solid balance at address and (2) by a bad grip of the club; usually a grip that emphasizes the right hand hold of the club instead of the proper connection which has the left hand holding a bit stronger.

When timing is thrown off badly by uncocking the wrists at the top of the backswing instead of at the latest possible moment that error is caused by a faulty grip, note the authorities. A feeling that the club is not under control at the top of the swing causes an instinctive grab at the club with the right hand.

Expert testimony adds up to good timing being an

especially vital element of golf because of the distance of the clubface from the player's hands, the varying speed of the body, arms and hands and the necessity of close precision in the vertical and horizontal angles of the clubface.

When the average golfer gets reading about the importance and delicacy of timing in golf he may feel hopeless and conclude that good timing is beyond his capabilities. But timing really isn't that abstruse. It is mainly a matter of patience; even of laziness. Take your time and you will get good timing on your golf shot. Hurry your shot and you take a big chance of being out of luck and skill.

"You don't see the ball eager to get on its way, do you?" an old pro asked his impatient pupil. "Don't rush. The ball will wait."

SHARPSHOOTING
AT
SHORT
RANGE

In the long twilight of summer in Scotland, the lads at Carnoustie entertained themselves pitching and putting. Occasionally there'd be bets made on hitting the big brass ball on top of the flagpole of the bandstand.

Carnoustie's principal and pleasant industry became exporting golf professionals to the American market. The Scotch Smiths had their brothers, Willie, Alex and Macdonald, migrate from Carnoustie to become as famous in the United States in golf as the American Smith brothers were in cough drops. The Clarksons and other golfing clans sent their merry missionaries.

The Carnoustie corps of professionals contributed greatly to the building of American golf. These pioneers weren't especially long hitters but in approaching they were deadly. Imitative American caddies, playing short holes they'd installed in the caddie corrals, absorbed the Carnoustie technique and put a polish of their own on it.

One of the American kids developed mastery of the short game that changed the policy of competitive golf. In the pre-Hagen days, a shot off the fairway meant a shot lost. Off the fairways then was tall and tangled rough, heavily infested with tough weeds and that's the sort of country that young Hagen and his contemporaries visited. It rarely flanks fairways at American golf courses now.

Somehow Hagen got the idea that instead of regarding a stray shot as inevitably costing a stroke there was nothing in the rules that said he couldn't shoot for the hole. The Haig would come out of the hay with a niblick (a 9-iron they call it now) or a mashie-niblick which was sort of a cross between today's 5-iron and 7-iron. He knocked the ball close enough to be in one-putt radius of the cup. That never-say-die program worked in stroke and match play. It worked then, and works now in the shrub-spotted "tiger country" framing British fairways.

Now, of course, with the wider fairways and rather short and well-groomed rough of American courses, and with the magic of the pitching and sand wedges, the expert who is on his game is fairly confident that he can get down in two shots from anywhere within 50 yards of the hole.

American caddies chipping and putting to holes they installed in the bare ground. Caddie corrals absorbed the Carnoustie (Scotch) technique and put a polish of their own on it.

RESCUE FROM THE ROUGH
Walter Hagen did not regard a stray shot as inevitably costing a stroke.
He shot for the green and sometimes made it.

Johnny Revolta was the middleman between the Hagen school and the modern pro short-range sharpshooters. Revolta, when 14, won the Wisconsin State Caddie championship with 312 which was a fine score on a brutal course in 1925. When he was about 17, he was pro at a nine-hole course where he had to stay close to the small pro shop, hence was working at his short game during his free time, which was plenty at that club.

Puzzled pros used to say that Johnny could hardly hit the ball out of his shadow but still he was beating everybody. He won the PGA championship in1935, beating

Armour in the final. That year he won the Western Open and was the PGA tour top money winner with $9,543, a sum that is won in one tournament now by professionals who come to Revolta to take post-graduate courses in the short game.

In his written advice on the subject, Johnny said for the ordinary golfer to develop chip and sand-trap wedge shots to a nearly fool-proof standard, all that has to be done is to acquire firmness, club head speed and timing.

So that's all there is to the department of the game that seldom is studied and practiced by the average fellows who go to the practice tees and bat out long shots, yet are lucky to get 190 to 210 yards when they're playing. The field generally gets about 240 yards or more off the tee in the National Open and PGA championships.

Tommy Armour, accurate, frank and acidulous in viewing golf and golfers, remarks that where the experts "murder" the second-raters and where amateurs who turn pro usually go hungry is in the short game. Armour adds that although any club member who has learned the first thing about playing golf must have noted the tremendous difference between the short game of the experts and that of the ordinary golfer, he has not met many common golfers who voluntarily seek instruction in chipping and pitching. Nor has he much seen many men or women golfers practicing shots of 30 or 40 yards or less.

FIRMNESS IN THE LEFT HAND

In explaining his formula of "firmness, clubhead speed and timing" for the short shots, Revolta says that by firmness he means firmness particularly in the left hand. His theory of playing the short shots well is based on keeping the left hand firm at impact so the face of the club can function as a projection of the palm of the

THE CHIPPING ART
Revolta's formula for chipping is, "firmness, particularly in the left hand, clubhead speed and timing." Both hands should be in a "strong" grip and active.

right hand. That, of course, calls for having the grip nicely adjusted and coordinated and for having the hands active rather than sluggish. He comments that he'd rather see the beginner grip the club with the right hand slightly underneath the shaft instead of on top as, when the back of the right hand is somewhat facing the sky, the right elbow is liable to fly off at a tangent.

FAST TEMPO ON SHORT SHOTS

Clubhead speed on the short shots, according to Revolta, must have a fast tempo and not the lazy, sloppy, scooping performance so often noticed. He recommends a brisk 1-2 cadence for the backswing, then a decisive downswing. There is no jerking or lunging at the ball but simply a swing so firm that the left hand doesn't collapse but goes through the shot.

A lot of golfers want backspin on their approach shots although it has been noted by experts that the ordinary golfer is short of the hole more than he is beyond it. Revolta in his short game opus says, "backspin is applied by swinging into the ball crisply and decisively, never allowing the left hand to collapse."

Revolta was the player most likely to succeed in getting out of traps, guarding greens and knocking the ball close to the hole. Horton Smith brought the wedge from an ingenious Texas amateur golfer into the factory of a major club manufacturer; Gene Sarazen developed the design, especially for use in sand traps, and Johnny Revolta showed them all how to use the club artistically.

GETTING OUT OF A TRAP

Revolta wasn't limited as a short game maestro to his use of the wedge in getting out of traps extraordinarily well. When the ball was lying well, the bank wasn't high and the hole was a goodly distance away, Revolta could chip about as close to the hole as most good ones could

GETTING OUT OF THE TRAP

For the normal sand shot lay the face of the club open. Hit down and through the sand two to three inches back of the ball, hands well ahead of the clubhead.

For a fast rising ball play the ball forward and keep the hands back of the ball at impact and perform an outside-in-plane, slicing under the ball.

For the buried ball, close the clubface so the toe of the club strikes the sand first, digs down into the sand and bumps the ball out.

94

lag a long putt. He once said, "When you're in a trap just off the green: On a chip shot you hit the ball first, then take sand; on an explosion you take sand before you hit the ball."

"The short shots are the tough babies for timing," Johnny emphasizes. "Timing comes from smoothness — smoothness is the backswing, the downswing, the follow-through. You can't take a quick short slap at the ball and call that timing."

In various phrases all of the authorities in teaching the short game say the same thing Revolta does about the importance of a strong left hand. The majority of the bad approach shots of the rank-and-file golfers are caused by the left wrist or left elbow collapsing and the right hand flipping the clubhead ahead of the hands. Then, as Armour observes, confusion is compounded by blaming the right hand for overpowering the left when what actually happened was that the left hand was weak.

Usually, the week-end golfer who is having trouble in hitting chip and pitch shots respectably, eases his right hand grip so he's barely holding onto the club yet doesn't improve any. He has failed to strengthen the grip of the last three fingers of his left hand.

WHERE TO STAND

There isn't the faintest suggestion of an argument about where to stand in relation to the ball, for the shorter shots. You simply stand with the ball to the right of the middle of your stance so your hands are ahead of the clubface. From this position you're bound to swing down so the clubhead gets well under the ball. The bottom of the arc of the swing is a bit ahead of the ball so when you take a divot it is in front of the ball.

Your left arm and the shaft of the club at address for a short shot are practically in a backward slanting line and, with the strong left wrist, they keep aligned through the shot.

PITCHING WITHOUT THE BODY

The pitches with the 8-9 iron or wedge are played with shoulder, arm and hand action: no body action other than that which comes gently as the result of freedom from tension.

The feet are only a few inches apart. The stance is slightly open. The open stance has a tendency to bring the clubface from outside the direction line in and across the line and developing a clockwise spin of the ball. That cut-shot effect tends to stop the shot shortly after it lights. That spin and the loft of the club reduce distance so the experts advise you to take a little more backswing than you might be disposed to take for a short shot. Another thing they all recommend is holding the club down on the grip but not too near the lower end of the grip material.

Without exception the foremost players and teachers say you've got to address the short shots with your weight accented on the left foot and you must keep it there all through the shot so you will be sure to hit down at the ball.

And you've got to stay steady. If your head moves perceptibly until after the ball is on its way, you probably will ruin your attempt. Stay down to the ball!

The chip shots are played when you're not far off the green and with a club that doesn't have much loft — anything from a 4- through a 6-iron is suggested to the average golfer, depending on how far he wants the ball to run after it hits the green. The experts, once in a while, will chip with a 7-iron. Stance for the chips is square. The shot is played virtually as a long putt, with the club held low on the grip, but ball played almost in line off the

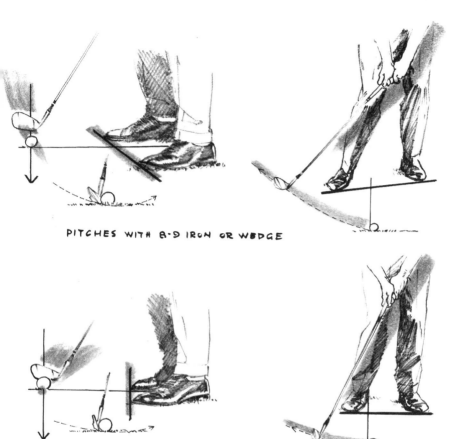

PITCHES WITH 8-9 IRON OR WEDGE

CHIP SHOTS WITH 4-5-6 IRONS

PITCHING AND CHIPPING

Pitch and chip shots accent a strong left hand. **For lofted pitches** take an open stance, break the wrists fast on the take away and come down into the ball sharply. **For low rolling chips** play from a square stance hold the wrists firm and keep the club low on the take away. **Backspin results from** the momentary contact of the ball with the clubface causing friction due to the speed and angle of the downward blow.

right toe, and not much wrist action. It calls for practically a pendulum swing.

Teaching specialists say that professional playing stars are apt to take for granted essentials they have so deeply ingrained that the details are like breathing or scratching where it itches.

Hence the headliners, according to the teachers, don't keep reminding the average players that the left elbow never must be allowed to bend until well after the ball is on its way, that the hands always should be kept comfortably close to the body and that the "sitting down" posture is the best way of assuring good steady balance in swinging into the ball. Those essentials are second nature to the man who has learned how to play well most of the time but they certainly aren't points the ordinary player remembers.

According to the teachers the typical golfer doesn't always recall that the club is designed to help him make the shot easily and surely so he ought to sole the club flat back of the ball then take his stance as dictated by the lie and the length of the club shaft. Something else that is primary but often neglected by the ordinary player is to keep the elbows feeling that they are being held comfortably together instead of being allowed to spread out as is so frequently the case with the careless player.

HOW TO EXPLOIT THE WEDGE

The wedge shot out of the bunker is the easiest of all shots in golf, if there is such a thing as the "easiest" shot, other than the conceded putt.

The formula for the wedge shot hasn't changed a bit since the first Esquire article on using the club: Hold the club near the end, the shot with an open stance with the ball off the right foot unless it is lying close to a steep bank and must be popped up quick, then it should be

THE FAIRWAY
From fairway traps, play the ball a little forward of normal so as to contact it at the lowest point of the arc. Aim a little to the left of your target line because a slight fade will result from the fact that the body pivot is restricted.

played off the left foot. In playing the wedge as in using any other club, keep the head steady; the wedge shot is an arm and hand shot with very little body in it — so simply accent weight on the left foot, keep the left arm straight, cock the wrists quickly in swinging the club away from the ball, and keep your right elbow down and close to you. Then when you hit an inch or two behind the ball (depending on the consistency of the sand) you must follow through so you won't leave the club buried in the bunker.

How much power you put into the wedge shot depends on how the sand is and how far the hole is from the ball. That's a matter of experience and feel. You have to learn that power answer for yourself. As usual, it's a matter of smooth timing, not of violent power.

Because the sand, not direct contact with the wedge clubface, takes the ball up and out of the traps, there is no spin on the ball. Consequently the open stance and the outside-in pull of the clubhead move the ball parallel to the front of the body. That requires an adjustment that seems to aim the ball somewhat to the right of the hole.

RESCUE FROM FAIRWAY TRAPS

In making shots out of fairway traps, if the lie is good and the bank of the bunker permits, use the same club you'd use from a fairway lie and be sure, emphasize the experts, to set your feet solidly, cock your hands fully at the top of the backswing and use lively hand action for the shot instead of making a stiff-wristed lunge at the ball.

One of the veteran teaching professionals adds that regardless of what is told the average golfer about playing a fairway trap shot, he always will try to get too much distance, take a club with less loft than is required and will bang the ball into the side of the bunker from which point it will dribble down to give the unhappy duffer another chance.

PITCHING FROM ROUGH OR FAIRWAY

The pitching wedge shots from fairway or rough are played with that club when the experts want to slide more of the club under the ball and pop it up and on its way with high trajectory. Two points that the mentors stress in playing these shots are: (1) While keeping the left hand strong, don't hold the club so tightly that wrist action is stiffened and (2) stand and hit down so the

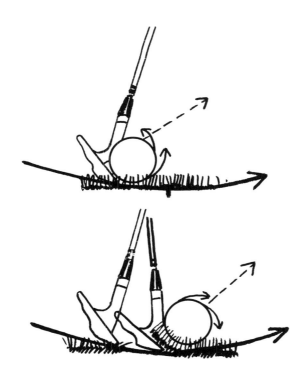

To get height and backspin control with a pitching wedge or other lofting iron, the low point of the arc must occur ahead of the ball. **Fairway explosion shot** from soft turf with a pitching wedge, will lob the ball high for a short distance. It will land with very little roll. Layer of turf between clubface and ball bumps ball *out* in clockwise spin.

---

leading edge of the club will come well under the ball and take the divot ahead of the ball.

The simple essential of getting the lowest part of the swing in the logical place for making the desired shot is mentioned, in one way or another, by all who tell about playing the bunker shots.

UPHILL, DOWNHILL, SIDEHILL
That point also is underlined in the texts on playing the uphill and downhill lies. On the uphill lies the ball is played a bit more than normal toward the left foot and the other way for downhill lies. Firm balance, of course,

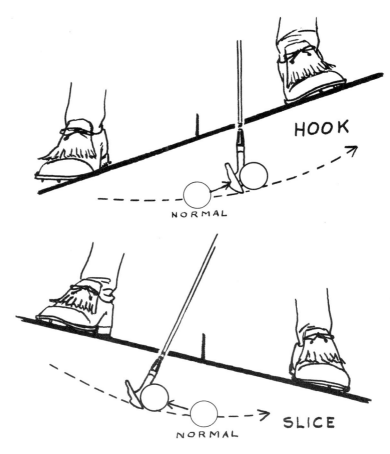

OFF THE HILL
In an uphill lie, play the ball forward toward the higher foot, with a straighter faced club. For downhill lie, play ball toward higher foot with a more lofted club.

---

is a major factor in playing the sidehill shots.

As the shots from uphill lies probably will be hooked you can play one number of a club weaker but should allow for a hook. For a slice, just the reverse is recommended. Hold the club at the end of the grip for a lie that's below the level of your feet and grip it shorter for a shot above the level of your stance. Any 24-handicap golfer who knows the first things about the ABC's of

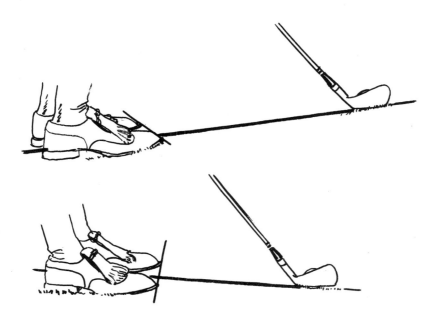

When the ball lies above the feet, the weight must be forward on the toes. The ball should hook. When the ball lies below feet, weight must be back on heels. The ball should fade.

golf—Address, Balance and Control, ought to be able to think out the right answers about making the shots from lies that aren't on lush, level, nicely manicured turf. Although the abnormal conditions often prevail in those curious places the ordinary golfer visits, he seldom learns that the most important thing about playing the recovery shots, as well as playing the shots that call for precision rather than power, is to think.

Several Esquire authorities testify that the most difficult thing to teach the common golfer is to think in the right way instead of getting himself tangled and cramped by merely thinking that he thinks.

PUTTING
IS
EASY
(IF YOU THINK IT IS)

"Putting is easy," said William Turnesa, the amateur of a fine, famous family of golf professionals.

Willie proclaimed his discovery during the United States Golf Association's Green Section meeting in New York, late in January 1964. His announcement was mildly sensational. It was the first time in the open history of golf that any national champion had declared that all there was to putting was rolling the ball on smooth turf into a hole close enough so an infant could reach it. The iron approach shots and the long wood shots were the difficult parts of the game, Mr. Turnesa asserted, and went into brief detail to fortify his statement.

Willie's discovery was made public after due deliberation. He won the U. S. Amateur championship in 1938 and 1948 and the British Amateur in 1947. It is not in the records or in anybody's recollection that our Willie had anything to say about the ease of putting shortly after he'd won those championships. He'd displayed considerable magic in knocking the ball out of bunkers close enough to holes to somewhat diminish the terror of the remaining putts.

But up to the time of the Turnesa pronouncement no golfer ever had dared to suggest that there was nothing tough about putting. In fact, the talk was all the other way: that putting was cruel and unusual punishment that should not be a part of a gentlemen's game. About every two or three months when he wanted to remind his sportswriter friends that the name was spelled "Sarazen", Gene used to propose that the cup be enlarged from 4¼ inches to 6 or 8 inches in diameter. The suggestion always was good for getting sports page space for golf on dull days and a few club tournaments were played with 6 inch holes but those experiments seemed to make no revolutionary difference in the game. The old ideal still springs out every other year or so but yet no sour soul has remarked that if the cup had been smaller a party other than Gene Sarazen would have won the U. S. National Opens of 1922 and 1932, the British Open in 1932 and the PGA championships of 1922, 1923 and 1933.

There was a year, 1915, when a hole ½ inch larger in diameter than the regulation 4¼ inches was used in a national championship; the National Amateur played at the Country Club of Detroit. It was won by Robert Gardner who defeated John G. Anderson, 5 and 4 in the final.

The discrepancy in the size of the cups wasn't discovered until 1954 when the National Amateur returned to the Country Club of Detroit and the course superintendent, in checking over old equipment and supplies in the course maintenance building, came across the cups that had been specially made for the championship 39 years prior. He happened to see the difference. Arnold Palmer won the 1954 Amateur, by a skinny margin. Palmer rolled the ball into regulation orifices to get 1-up victories in the first, second, fifth, semi-final and final round when he beat Bob Sweeny.

However, even back in American golf's paleozoic time of 1915 the larger cup didn't seem to make much difference. The medalist score at Detroit that year was 152, made by Dudley Mudge who lost in the first round. The medalist score the previous year when the Amateur was played at Ekwanok Country Club, Manchester, Vt., was

144. Co-medalists were R. R. Gorton and W. C. Fownes, Jr. Fownes beat Gorton in the third round then in a semifinal round lost to Francis Ouimet, the eventual winner.

Despite the Amateur at Ekwanok being played with the regulation 4¼ inch diameter holes, you can safely guess that it wasn't entirely the putting that accounted for Ekwanok's medalist figure being 8 strokes easier over the 36 holes than the low qualifying score at the Country Club of Detroit.

In 1916 when the National Amateur was played at the Merion Cricket Club in suburban Philadelphia, W. C. Fownes, Jr., was medalist with 153 and you can be fairly positive, even this far away, that old Merion back then was more than a half-stroke a round harder than the Country Club of Detroit course in 1915. The 1916 Amateur was won by Chick Evans who qualified at 158. A 14-year-old named Bobby Jones, who later was to write on golf for Esquire and attain even greater distinction, qualified at 163.

So those championships before and after the year of the Big Cup do not appear to have proved that a small difference in the size of the hole makes a large difference in the quality of the putting.

Regulation size of the hole was accidentally determined at St. Andrews and from there spread with unquestioned acceptance. The old custom was to take a pinch of sand out of the hole for teeing up the ball a couple of club lengths away from the hole just played. Soon the holes got wide and deep and caved in. The first — and for a long time, the only — maintenance work done manually on a golf course was that of the man hired to dig new holes.

Two Scots got the idea of lining a caved-in hole on the Old Course at St. Andrews with a piece of clay drain tile they saw not far away. That pipe happened to be 4¼

A stray piece of clay drain tile. This incident determined the size of the hole: 4¼ inches in diameter.

inches in diameter. The first mention of standard dimensions for the hole was in Royal and Ancient Code of 1891.

Now the rules call for having the hole 4¼ inches in diameter and at least 4 inches deep. If a lining be used it shall be sunk at least 1 inch below the putting green surface.

When a fellow wins you don't hear him complain

about the size of the cup. In winning the 1964 National Open Ken Venturi averaged 31 putts per round; five putts per round lower than the figure the United States Golf Association considers the "error-less play" of an expert golfer.

The British Golf Union's Standard Scratch Score and Handicapping Scheme had an equivalent of par that calls for a scratch player taking not more than 35 putts for 18 holes. It is to be doubted that the standard of British greens is any better than that of greens in the United States although natural climatic and, sometimes, soil conditions at the better English and Scotch courses favor excellent putting surfaces.

In further support of the Turnesa statement that putting is easy is the historic performance of Willie Park, Jr., winner of the British Open in 1887 and 1890 on greens that certainly couldn't have approached the perfection of today's typical American greens.

Willie, Jr. was the last of the great Scottish match players. They played for what was big money in the 1850's, '60's, '70's and '80's. It was their own money. They didn't need any sponsors. Willie's sire, Willie, Sr., had a challenge for 20 years in a sporting paper, Bell's Life, London, to play any other man in the world for 100 pounds a side. Old Willie won the first British Open in 1860, and again in 1863, 1866 and 1875. His brother, Mungo, won it in 1874.

Willie, Jr. practiced putting eight hours a day. He was deadly when six feet from the hole. He designed many courses in the United States. Overwork from his golf architecture resulted in his death. Park Jr., had the idea that golf course design started with greens and went backward to the tees. Getting onto some of his intriguingly trapped greens was difficult enough, then when you got on the greens, the whole placement may have provided another problem.

The Park influence on golf course design, though not Park's actual work, is reflected in the Olympia Fields (suburban Chicago) course on which Johnny Farrell beat Bob Jones in a play-off for the 1928 National Open championship. Before Farrell got to him Jones was whipped by the par 3 holes. He went for the pins and wound up in bunkers and that generally meant losing a stroke in the pre-wedge days.

Don't ever think that Jones wasn't a heavenly putter a good part of the time. He holed them when he needed them. Even the short ones.

Holing the long ones at critical times isn't too rare. You're not disgraced if you miss so there's no undue pressure on you as there is when you've got a 20 inch putt to win—and a disturbing idea for each inch.

Those deceptive slopes on putts under three feet murder you. Tommy Armour has a policy about them that will pay you a lot more than this book cost you. The perennially youthful Silver Scot says there very rarely is a "borrow" on any putt under three feet. Holing such putts is simply a matter of rolling the ball at the center of the cup at the correct speed.

THE SHORT PUTT
In putting around three feet aim firmly for the center of the cup. Any drift that may normally occur will have so little effect that the ball will drop.

Sam Snead probably is the most successful holer of long putts golf has ever seen. When Sam won the world Senior Professional Championship in 1964 that made his 125th championship. The only reason the National Open isn't included in that list is because Sam got thinking the short putts are agonizingly tough and when you think that, they are.

Bob Jones told in his book "Down the Fairway" that he used to have several putting methods in a round after he'd started by missing a few putts he thought he should have made. Jones was an exceptionally smart golfer, so smart that he did not out-smart himself but logically examined what happened and why.

Jones with "Calamity Jane" as his weapon putted holes through the opposition's hearts. Only one man, the ex-schoolmaster Willie Macfarlane, out-putted Jones head-on, and that was in 1925 during a double-header play-off in the National Open at the Worcester (Mass.) CC after they'd tied at 291, seven over par, tied again at four over par with 75s, then after being four strokes behind Jones in the first nine of the second play-off Macfarlane squeezed through with 72, one less than Jones.

Macfarlane used to say that when he could hold the putter gently he would putt very well but the least bit of tightening his grip ruined him. Maybe it was mental tension, primarily, that changed putting from the easy job Willie Turnesa discovered it is, to a rough task. But that you'll have to decide for yourself as putting, whether or not it's easy, is the department of golf that permits and requires a wide scope of individual expression.

In Autumn of 1933, Jones wrote what became one of the minor classics of golf instruction.

He began his Esquire treatise of "The Art of Putting"

The Bobby Jones putting technique began with a comfortable relaxed grip and stance.

by observing the importance of individuality, hence the artistic character, in putting technique, by saying:

"There is great danger in adopting a method that is too nearly fixed and immutable. Too often a man who attempts to copy each detail of the style of someone else, or who tries to develop his own method according to rigid specifications, finds himself entirely tied up by the tension of his position. I should like one who reads this to understand that there is to be allowed some latitude for the individual in order to assure complete comfort and relaxation.

"In order that we may begin with a semblance of a proper sequence, we may divide the important fundamentals of putting into three headings. First, the correct grip; second, the position at address; and, third, the stroke itself.

START WITH THE THUMBS

"I think that the best way to bring out what I consider to be the chief requirements of the grip would be to describe my own and give the reasons for the appearance of the important features. In the first place, the thumbs of both hands touch the club exactly on the top of the shaft. This accomplishes two things. It locates my two hands with respect to each other and with respect to the face of the club in what I deem to be the proper position, that is, with the back of the left hand presented squarely to the hole and the palm of the right hand, if it were opened, in the same position. This is intended to encourage a stroke directed exactly along the line of the putt and to discourage a tendency of either hand to twist the face of the club away from its proper alignment.

"The grip should always be light.

"The nice correlation of direction and speed, which is so necessary to successful putting, demands a very deli-

cate touch and there is nothing which can defeat this so completely as a tense grip. My grip on a putter could be called firm only in the three smaller fingers of my left hand. My right hand merely rests upon the club as I am addressing the ball.

THE REVERSE LITTLE FINGER — FOREFINGER OVERLAP

"I suppose my grip would be called a reverse overlap, that is, instead of the ordinary overlapping grip, in which the little finger of the right hand overlaps the forefinger of the left hand, in this case the forefinger of the left hand is on top. The advantage of this, I think, in addition to encouraging a light grip, is to remove the possiblity of squeezing the shaft of the club between the thumb and forefinger of the left hand, a tendency which would be increased by the firmness of the grip of the smaller fingers of this hand.

"One of the chief dangers in putting, just as in playing every other golf shot, is that of raising the club too abruptly in starting the backswing, a motion which is usually accomplished by the right hand. The putter, like any other club, should be started back close to the ground and should never pass outside of an imaginary line drawn through the ball to the hole. I have found that the best way to prevent this is to start the backswing by means of the small fingers of the left hand, in which I have said that the grip was firm.

LEFT HAND, DIRECTION — RIGHT HAND, TOUCH

"As accurately as I can describe the feeling, the putting stroke is to me a matter of using the left hand for direction and true contact and the right hand for touch and speed. The firmness in the left hand controls the path of the putter blade and the delicate sense between the thumb and forefinger of the right hand makes the last little adjustment in the strength of the blow and

gives it its crisp quality.

"There is one very important point which concerns the way in which the right thumb makes contact with the club. It will be seen that only the first joint of this thumb is touching the club. The grip at this point, as a matter of fact, is very light and the control is as delicate as possible. Many fine putters look upon this as the secret of their ability to accurately gauge the speed of a fast green. A few, notably Johnny Farrell, make the contact with only the end of the thumb and press the thumb nail into the leather of the grip. Any number of bad putters, particularly beginners, press the whole length of this thumb upon the shaft. They thereby lose all sense of touch in that area.

"I think this about disposes of the particular features of the grip which I think are important.

"There is not likely to be a necessity for much variation from the orthodox. Some players will, no doubt, find that the reverse overlap is not comfortable for them. In this case they should by no means use it.

SACRIFICE ALL FOR COMFORT

"The most sensible thing which could be said about the proper address for the putt is that every possible consideration should be sacrificed to comfort; and as I have said before, the thing which prevents this most often is the attempt to reproduce exactly the method of someone else. There is no possibility of putting well without a rhythmic stroke, directed by relaxed muscles, capable of receiving the most delicate impulses. To studiously imitate in all respects the attitude of another player, immediately sets up a strain or tension which makes smooth stroking impossible. No matter how great or how perfect may be the model, his posture cannot be the easiest and most comfortable for everyone.

"I have been through all this myself so I think I am qualified to speak. No one could have had more worry in developing a reliable putting method than I have. In the various stages of my labor I have tried to imitate the styles of nearly all the great putters—tried to make myself look like them and given myself, as nearly as possible, the same mannerisms—and in the end I became unalterably convinced that the attempt to imitate was itself the most serious mistake I was making. Now, I never give a thought to the placing of my feet, to the inclination or the facing of my body, nor to anything else except assuring a definitely affirmative answer to the question, 'Am I comfortable?'

"It is for the same reason that I should never consider for a moment advising a person to keep his head still or his body immovable. Whether or not the best putters do *stand perfectly still while making the stroke has nothing to do with it. The point is that trying to do these things produces tension and tension must be avoided. I should always advise to forget these things entirely, and to allow them to take care of themselves. If the motion of the swing suggests the necessity of a slight movement of the body then by all means let it move. The feeling of ease and comfort thus gained is worth all the mechanical perfection that could be crammed into a dozen strokes. Rhythm and smoothness—smoothness and rhythm—these are the two things most desired.*

POSITIONING THE FEET

"Now to be a little more specific—I find that is is an aid to comfort to stand with my feet quite close together, just as I would stand normally if I were not playing a golf shot, to permit a slight bend in both knees, and to keep my arms close to my body. Perhaps, since the word 'keep' connotes the exercise of some restraint, it would

*be better to say that I refrain from extending my arms
away from my body.*

*"My elbows each show a considerable bend. This
attitude is the one which I find the most comfortable, and
the one which best encourages ease and relaxation. I
may say that there is at least nothing about it which is
at all studied or artificial.*

A SWEEP — NOT A SMACK

*"I think the best conception to have of the putting
stroke itself is that it should be a long sweep. I like to
feel that, instead of driving the ball toward the hole, I
am merely sweeping it, or bowling it over the green. The
two important characteristics of the stroke which this
kind of picture induces are first, a marked flatness of
the arc — the blade of the putter never rises abruptly
either going back or following and second, a good alignment which prevents cutting across the ball. The in-
tention to sweep rather than hit tends to prevent a
pick-up with the right hand, which is the chief cause of
cutting. If the club be swung back mainly with the left
hand, there is little danger of lifting, and the head of the
putter will always remain well on the inside, whence a
stroke directed along the intended line of the putt can be
accomplished.*

THE ARMS — CLOSE BUT LOOSE

*"I have said that the arms should be close to the body.
This is true, but there should never be any suggestion
that the player is 'hugging himself.' In my own style
my right forearm is lightly touching the front of my
trousers, but I am always careful to see that my left arm
is entirely free. If this elbow is pressed close against the
left side untold trouble can result, for there is thus encouraged an almost irresistible tendency to yank the
putt off line to the left.*

"Whenever I begin to notice a tendency to pull my putts, and feel a tightening in the left wrist as I hit the ball, I turn this left elbow even farther out until at times it is pointing almost directly toward the hole. This overcomes to a great extent the locking tendency and encourages again a stroke along the proper line.

LONG BACKSWING HELPS SMOOTHEN STROKE

"Many players run into trouble on the greens because they are afraid to trust a backswing which is long enough to allow a smooth stroke without hurry or effort.

"The inclination is very strong, particularly when trying to hole a difficult six-footer, to figure that the shortest possible backswing runs the least danger of turning the club away from the proper setting. In my own case, at least, this has been utterly disproved. I find that my troubles only multiply when I shorten my backswing —that then I begin to jab, stab and cut, and that very soon any semblance of touch has vanished. An ample backswing, leisurely and free, not only makes my putting stroke mechanically better, but it serves also to keep me in a much better state of mind, where I am able to concentrate upon hitting the ball correctly instead of worrying about irregularities and hidden rolls in the green."

And that concluded the putting gospel according to Jones. Maybe there have been better putters than Bobby, but how do you know?

The old gentleman who tried to make a science of putting, Mark G. Harris, was an early contributor to Esquire with his system of putting mechanics.

Harris took up golf in his 60's. He wanted to show that an older man could master the game. He never got so he could hit the ball much over 150 yards but he was down in two from anywhere on a fairway or medium rough from 50 yards out.

He summarized successful putting technique:

(1) A grip that gives the player delicacy of touch, firmness without stiffness and which, at address, has the back of the left hand parallel with the face of the putter and facing the hole;

(2) A square stance, knees bent, the eyes directly over the ball, the sole of the putter flat on the ground at address;

(3) A slow, low backswing with the upper half of the right arm sliding against the body as the putter is swung into the ball;

(4) Keeping the head absolutely motionless.

Harris was a cocky, dapper old chap who delighted in exhibiting his approaching and putting ability. He thought the short game should be easy for anyone who followed his directions.

Claude Harmon, writing much later than Harris, in Esquire, said, "There are as many effective styles (of putting) as there are golfers." Nevertheless, Harmon declared that a golfer could be taught to be a good putter and a technique developed to assure greater accuracy.

Harmon's points for generally satisfactory putting included a few "musts":

(1) A relaxed, comfortable stance;

(2) A comfortable light grip that keeps the hands in line usually with both thumbs running down the center of the shaft;

(3) The putter must be kept low to the ground in the backswing, which determines the distance the putt is to go, and low and square to the line of the putt, in the follow-through;

(4) The head and body must remain motionless all during the stroke, to provide the immovable framework that is a fulcrum for the arms in making the backward and

forward swing;

(5) Fix the line of the putt in your mind so you will know what you've got to do and will have confidence you can do it.

Horton Smith was one of golf's uniformly good putters for many years. He had a questioning mind. He listened to his professional colleagues complain about the putts they should have had. He got the feeling that pros are disposed to over-emphasize putting.

Then he went into his Esquire script: "If I Could Only Putt." Said the observant Smith:

"The fellow having the least distance to putt does the best putting.

"The tournament experts in the last few years have been putting better because they have paid more attention to approaching and chipping that brings them into position for easier putts. They see to it now that they get straight-away or uphill putts rather than the risky, difficult taps that must roll downhill or make a very accurate 'borrow' from a side-hill location.

"Consequently, when you hear tournament players talk about marvelous putting you probably are hearing only part of the story. The part about the approach shot is the part that's not often mentioned.

"Of course, putting is better than it used to be. Greens are much truer than they used to be. Golfers can thank greenkeepers for that part of the improvement. Approach areas, due to fertilizing and fairway watering, provide much better lies for either long or delicate approach shots. Again, the players must acknowledge their debt to the greenkeepers. But where a great part of the reputed improvement in putting has originated is with the wedge type of niblick.

"I know that times without number I have used this sort of club to get from a sand trap tightly guarding a

*green close enough to the hole to have the easiest kind
of a putt left.*

*"Still I don't want to think that I am such a great put-
ter that when I miss one I should be upset and immediately begin experimenting with some different putting
method.*

*"I believe I had more favorable conditions for estab-
lishing a putting technique than most of the professionals have had. I started playing on sand greens.
Those greens, necessarily, were level and the ball left
a line behind it as it was putted. I learned to hit the ball
true because I could analyze from the track the putted
ball left on the sand green just what had been wrong
with the way the putt was hit.*

*"As an amateur, early in my competitive experience, I
played in the Missouri State tournament against Clarence Wolf, who then was one of the finest amateurs in
the Midwest. I was on the green in practically the same
number of shots as Clarence but he finished with a 74
to my 84. It wasn't very hard for me to account for the
difference. I went back home and practiced putting
until the mechanics of putting became set with me.
I haven't had to bother with mechanical details of putting to any extent since that time, but the mental details are always hazardous.*

*"When I started on my first and extremely fortunate
winter tournament trip I was happily ignorant of the
perils of tricky 'borrows' and grains of ingeniously con-
toured grass greens. I didn't realize they were much
more difficult to putt than the flat sand greens I'd been
playing on. So without being scared or bewildered I
putted only for the line I figured would put my ball into
the hole. Older and more experienced players had
missed a lot of putts thrown off a line by a grass grain
that ran the wrong way or by a slight slope they didn't*

observe. *They naturally approached their putts with that nervous feeling of angels fearing to tread. By the time I became experienced enough to associate the psychological advantage I had over them I had passed the critical period of possible stage fright.*

"There is far from the difference in putting ability amongst the foremost professionals there'd have to be to give foundation to the belief that tournament golf has become merely a series of putting contests.

"Our players concentrate on method and form of all shots and on competitive attitude. If any of us has some improved and more certain putting method you may depend on others who are trained, vigilant and keen observers finding out the secret and making it generally known soon. It's strictly a business with us.

"My own opinion is that putting publicity rather than putting performance has always been responsible for tending to implant the erroneous idea that putting is away out of balance with respect to the rest of the game. I even have the hunch that publicity has made or ruined many good putters to a degree that players themselves don't realize."

THE
ART OF
LEARNING
AS YOU
PLAY

What now is called a "playing lesson" with the tutor playing the course with the pupil, until about 1900 was the only method of golf instruction. The pupil, usually a well-do-do Scot or Englishman on a holiday, had as his tutoring playing companion a graduate caddie who had gone into clubmaking then, because of his aptitude at playing and his understandable eagerness to make money at what he liked to do for nothing, got odd jobs as accompanist to vacation visitors.

The lesson tee for specializing in instruction was a development that started to become popular in the United States in the first decade of the twentieth century. At the British Clubs the early professional was the club and ballmaker, greenkeeper, starter, caddiemaster, playing companion, head caddie and instructor in the order named. As the game grew he had to limit the scope of his duties. His first teaching was in some specialized performance such as showing the beginner how to get out of the cavernous, unraked sandy wastes that were the bunkers of the links on the Scotch shores. That was quite a trick in the pre-wedge days. After chopping a niblick at balls in the sand for, maybe a half hour or as much less or longer as the student and instructor could stand the experiments, the lesson was completed.

Some golf enthusiasts who had money and time to throw away would take lessons on how to whack a ball out of a divot gash. The idea that the player could pick up the ball and place it in a greatly improved lie, when he didn't like where the ball had rolled, didn't occur to the earlier golfers. They thought golf was supposed to be played by hitting it, not carrying it, from one place to another. It is peculiar that the practice of lifting the ball onto a practically teed-up spot developed in the United States at courses where even bad fairways are better than most of the fairways on famed Scotch, English, Irish and French courses.

Older Scotch-American professionals have commented that what's prevented the average American golf club member from learning how to hit a good shot is the practice of teeing the ball up on the slightest excuse, thus encouraging a scoop or a sweep at the ball instead of hitting down into the ball as a shot should be played.

That observation might bring up the reflection that as golf is played on golf courses, on golf course is where golf should be learned. However, shortage of time of the instructors available and in some cases the crowds of players on the courses prevented growth of the playing lesson procedure.

Golf instruction books had a great deal to do with creating the demand for professional instruction. The earliest books, of course, were written by thinking amateurs. The first "best seller" of golf books was "Golf" of the Badminton Library which was edited, and to a considerable extent written, by Horace G. Hutchinson, who was runner-up to A. F. MacFie in the first British Amateur championship (1885) and who won that championship in 1886 and 1887, and was runner-up again in 1902. There were contributions by Sir Walter Simpson, Right Hon. A. J. Balfour, Lord Wellwood and others. it was published in London in 1890 and appeared in many later editions. Hutchinson also edited and largely wrote "The Book of Golf and Golfers" which was published in 1899. It contained scholarly contributions by Miss M. Pascoe, winner of the 1896 Ladies British championship and by H. H. Hilton, amateur who won the British Open in 1892 and 1897, the British Amateur in 1901, 1911 and 1913 and the U. S. Amateur in 1911. Another contributor was H. J. Whigham who won the American Amateur championships in 1896 and 1897. J. H. Taylor, the studious and literate winner of the British Opens of 1894, 1895, 1900, 1909 and 1913 and the 1900 U. S. Open, was another contributor in that book. It didn't take Harry Vardon long to come out with his book "The Complete Golfer." His first edition came out shortly after the turn of the century and it was having its 12th edition in the U. S. in 1912. Henry Leach was Vardon's literary caddie and a fine job he did of getting Vardon to "tell all" as Vardon was not what anybody would call a gassy guy.

The early golf instruction books sold very well in the United States and fired up enthusiasm for building courses and hiring professionals. When the professionals came to take the new jobs they found that showing a fellow how and where to mow the greens, where to have the horse haul the mower to separate fairways from rough, and either making enough clubs themselves or teaching the brighter caddies to do it, ruled them out of teaching by playing lessons, hence the instruction tee plan got to be nearly universal in golf instruction of Americans.

Now and then, if a club member is lucky, he will be able to get a playing lesson of nine or even 18 holes on his own course with his own professional. The professional takes a risk. Somebody else may come to the pro shop and ask to be given a lesson and when told that the professional is out playing with another member may think the pro is favoring his pets. The suspicion is silly, of course, but it has made some professionals wary of giving playing lessons when their lesson tee time is pretty well booked.

Embarrassment of the high-handicap players is another reason that the playing lessons have sharply deminished. The player who does not play well is afraid or ashamed—or both—to play with a professional for a playing lesson, a friendly round or in a pro-amateur affair. This nervous attitude is unnecessary. The intelligent, well-bred professional regards the amateur in this case as a client of professional golf and a source from which all blessings flow.

"The amateur could be no worse at golf business than I probably would be at his," comments Charley Penna, a representative first class professional at a first class club. Penna also reassures the amateur who plays in the pro-amateur affairs by saying that the pro usually is thinking so much about his own game and his responsibility of making every shot look good to his amateur partner that he hasn't any time to spare in worrying about mistakes the amateur has to make.

Although the lesson tee manner of teaching enables the competent professional to give individual attention to more pupils, and allows the pupils to get specialized instruction on which they and the instructor can concentrate, it has one serious defect. It teaches the student to make golf shots but doesn't teach him to play golf.

Golf is played on a golf course, not on a lesson tee or at a golf range.

The course is the part of the game that tests the player's judgment, his knowledge of tactics, his acquaintance with his clubs and his mental capacity to out-think his opponent in match play, or the rest of the field in stroke play, and to discover whether he has as much brains as the golf course architect. He may discover that the man who planned the golf course is a crafty party and took advantage of what nature, primarily, had done to make golf interesting and testing.

The golfer has to learn something about golf beyond hitting the ball before he becomes aware of the inherent fascination of the game. He may have known plenty about baseball, football, tennis and basketball. They are played on areas of uniform dimensions. When he gets into golf where every course is different and rarely are two holes identical he begins to realize that he is playing a game that has a unique challenging factor; the course.

And, to record the belief of many professionals who know amateurs better than the amateur golfers know themselves, only about one player out of ten knows the slightest thing about how to use brains in playing a golf course. That's a harsh indictment but realistic professionals are tough on their own kind and maintain that there are dozens of splendid shotmakers on the practice tees at tournaments who get out on the course and make inexcusably ignorant tactical errors.

Time after time the golf club member whose handicap is 12 or higher will play his home course and have a shot left to a green without knowing from any landmark (except a 150 yards out marker on some courses) what distance he's got to make, even though there are conspicuous natural markers that would have helped him had he really studied his course.

LEARNING HOW TO "READ" THE COURSE
Gene Andrews, a California amateur good enough to play in Walker cup competition, devised a sort of a shorthand system of reading golf courses and recording them on scorecards. His system helped him get the most

out of his game. Jack Nicklaus in playing practice rounds had an adaptation of the Andrews' idea that he penciled in on scorecards and that has kept the canny Nicklaus from wasting years and shots that usually are thrown away by young fellows who are fooled by golf courses.

Wind, nature of the grass and the ground, wetness or dryness of the ground, trees that shut off wind or cast shadows that make distance deceptive, rough that may be thick near fairways because of the sprinklers' sweep and thin farther out, trap sand that may be powdery or coarse, fairway bunkers that may be higher than the adjacent fairway or which may have the fairway sloping down toward them, design that may have most out-of-bounds to the left (or right), greens that present danger-ous three-putt risks unless you hit them with foresight — those are but a few of the multitude of golf architectural factors to which Esquire's teachers referred in relating their competitive trials and troubles.

Unfortunately, the average golfer seldom gets enough chance to play courses with seasoned professionals and learn why the holes are designed as they are and how the hazards can be avoided by the player, regardless of ability, who uses his head. There is a wide variation in golf course design notions but all golf architects who are entitled to be called "architects" agree that the golfer who is penalized by inability to get much dis-tance should not be further punished by a hazard that he cannot escape by thoughtfully directing his line of play.

The long course isn't too often the good one because many times it can be played with a strong back and a weak mind, by the old and frequently true, analysis.

No bad hole is made any better by having the tee set back farther. Now, almost any golfer who can break 100 considers himself a golf architect, and the grotesque revisions of golf holes by golf club Green committees shows how extravagant this delusion of golf architectural knowledge can be. It will be noted that a high percentage of the famous golf holes on older courses were made by the architect seeing where nature had provided a superb green, then working back from there. You will see in tournament programs that holes are described as "tee shot" holes or "second shot" holes but canny campaigners regard nearly all holes, except very few par 5s as second shot holes because the second shot demands a higher degree of proficiency than the drive, particularly where the fairways are reasonably wide and the rough isn't severe from 230 to 250 yards from the tee markers, the average range of the professional and low handicap amateur drive.

The problem of the club member in trying to learn how to play his own course may be complicated if his course is a new one that has been designed to test the tournament professionals who don't pay dues at the club and seldom play the course. It is ridiculous but the truth is that quite a few of the costlier newer courses are designed for strong, expert golfers who never will play them. But that's golf the way it is today. Many club dues payers have to discover for themselves how to play their own courses.

SELECTING AND FITTING THE CLUBS

Something else that is a neglected part of education in golf and which has been but briefly mentioned in the Esquire treatises is the subject of clubs.

The importance of perfectly fitted clubs has been referred to as the governing factor in hitting the ball well. Teaching authorities have estimated that the 85-shooter wastes at least three shots a round because he doesn't know how to play the course and four shots a round because he uses the wrong clubs. Correcting those errors would give the slightly better than average golfer a normal round of 78. The number of shots misplayed because of ignorance of how to play the course or how to choose the club for the shot increases or decreases in ratio to a player's customary score.

PLAYING WITH THE RULES

Although there is the common belief that the rules cost the ordinary player strokes (or would if he played golf instead of whatever the game is that he plays when he makes his own rules) the rules frequently help the player. When he is playing as a guest at a course he doesn't know he ought to read the local rules on the back of the scorecard as they may tell him of situations that might normally cost him penalties when playing at his own course and with fellows who won't stand for his casual interpretation of the Rules of Golf.

For instance: Often around new plantings a local rule may allow a "free lift." Where there are an abnormal number of out-of-bounds risks or situations in which the stroke and distance penalty would be unduly severe, the United States Golf Association says that a local rule reducing the penalty might be advisable. The lighter penalty suggested is dropping a ball, under penalty of one stroke, within two club-lengths of the place where the ball last crossed the boundary line.

The uninformed golfer, wanting to play fair but not knowing the rules, may handicap himself by trying to play a ball that's close to an obstruction such as a sprinkler head, although the rules allow him to lift the ball and drop it within two club-lengths not nearer the hole. Roads are not obstructions but local rules sometimes ease the situation and with the many miles of golf car roads on which golf balls come to rest players ought to check on local rules.

Probably the one rule most frequently violated is 33, prohibiting soling a club in a hazard.

At many private clubs women golfers know and observe the rules more than men do. The women's golf committees have their rules educational sessions with the rules book, the professional and, usually the "Golf Rules in Pictures" book prepared by Joseph C. Dey, Jr., of the U.S.G.A., to clarify the rules and their application. Hundreds of golf clubs supply their members each year with copies of "The Rules of Golf" booklets. Copies of the book are available from the United States Golf Association, 40 East 38th St., New York, N. Y., 10016, at a cost of 25 cents each when fewer than 500 are ordered.

Repeated stories tell how championships were won by tactics that involved wise use of the rules, outsmarting the architect and by heroic and lucky or successful shots at desperate moments. Horton Smith's victory in a Masters tournament by canny use of the rule allowing escape from casual water on a green is one of the tactical cases in point.

Tommy Armour counseled average golfers to be intelligent enough to think one shot ahead then deliberately play the easiest shot immediately required. Armour's reminders to the golfer that he could save himself strokes by thinking of the reward or punishment potential in the course architecture were so helpful that they suggested a literary substitute for the practical tuition of the playing lesson.

There were a number of applications of this instruction made by tournament professionals as members of amateur-pro teams. The results generally presented the tactics of a guy who could knock a drive 260 yards with a curve of direction as circumstances required; who could open or shut the face of a club to finesse a shot out of the rough; who could splash out of the sand to within "gimme" distance of the hole or who could figure our delicate borrows of green contour; "grain" of the greens grass, speed of the greens as influenced by moisture at the particular time of the day and other such details. This advice was over the head of the average golfer.

SPECIAL
HINTS
FOR
SPECIFIC
PROBLEMS

The typical golfer who goes to the first tee of a course usually is stiff and embarrassed. Naturally, he will take a cramped, quick and incomplete swing and slice or push the ball to the right. If out-of-bounds, shrubs, trees or hazards are fairly close to the right of the fairway the golfer beginning his round will be off to a bad start and lose a stroke unless he tees up his ball to the right of the teeing area and aims to the left where he will have a lot of comfortably safe landing area for his initial drive.

Carelessness in aiming as well as thoughtlessness in not determining where to aim throw away strokes for the typical golfer. Every time the rules allow the expert will sole his club back of the ball so the lower and leading edge of the club squarely across the direction line gives him the primary element of a precision aim. Everything else — stance, posture, hand placement — is adjusted to that aim.

CORRECT CLUB FOR THE CORRECT TRAJECTORY

A common error of the average golfer is to be short in lofting a ball intended to land on the green but dropping down into a trap. This isn't necessarily the result of a mistake in selecting a club that hasn't got enough distance for an 8- or 9-iron or wedge easily will pop the shot out of the rough or from a fairway as far as it needs to go. What causes the trouble is that the player is unmind-

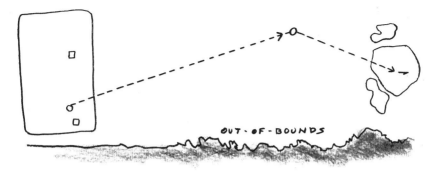

STRATEGY ON THE TEE
When hazards are close to the right of the fairway, tee on the same side as trouble and aim away from it.

ful of the trajectory of the shot being so high that it kills distance. Too late the victim remembers he should have swung back a little farther and hit a little harder.

Another blunder that tosses away strokes is taking a club of too much loft and pitching a shot that bumps into the inclined face of a green and stops far short of the hole when the same shot played as an easy chip with a 5-, 6- or even 7-iron would have rolled up the bank and close to the hole.

OUT OF THE FAIRWAY, INTO THE FOREST

When the typical golfer is playing on a course that has fairways framed by trees it is almost a sure thing that he is going to be playing several shots out of a forest. At least one of them will cost him a stroke or two because he will take a club with too much loft and hit the ball into one or more of the lower branches. The safe and good shot probably would have been easy had he taken a 4-iron, played the ball to the right of center of his stance, and hit down with lively hand action.

If he gets the ball out of the woods — anywhere out of

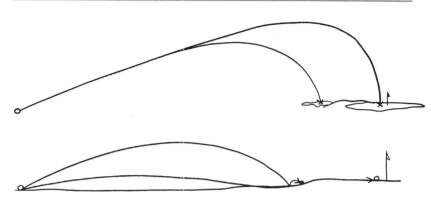

LOFTED CLUBS
Hit firmer with a lofted club since height takes away some distance.

Play a club that will keep the ball safely under all branches.

the woods—he possibly is lucky as then he will be past the danger of slamming the ball against a tree and having it rebound and hit him in the head. The panicky shots frequently have the ordinary player lunging at the ball and as there is no steadiness of aim or execution there is no telling where the ball will go. The most brainless thing a so-called golfer can do is to risk knocking an eye out by playing a risky shot in the woods.

DECIDING WHEN A BALL IS PLAYABLE

In the woods or any place else the player is sole judge as to whether his ball is unplayable. If he decides that the ball is unplayable he can play his next stroke as nearly as possible at the spot from which the original ball was played, adding a penalty stroke to his score. He has the alternative of dropping a ball, under penalty of one stroke, either within two club-lengths of the point where the ball lay, but not nearer the hole, or behind the point where the ball lay, keeping that point between himself and the hole, with no limit to how far behind that point the ball may be dropped.

Where there are carries over water that may be too perilous for the capacity of a player there invariably are safer routes that allow the cautious player to go for a one-putt par. Maybe it's cowardly but the 5s on the par 3 holes murder the ordinary golfer who is afraid to use his head. The old line about the scorecard telling "how many" and not "how" should inspire the golfer who is shrewd enough to play the club he knows he can play most reliably.

DETERMINING WHAT CLUB DOES WHAT

Using a putter to rap a ball so it rolls over the sand, up the bank and onto the green isn't spectacular but it certainly isn't illegal and is as safe as a wedge shot or safer, usually, than a delicate chip out of a trap. But who

The "Texas wedge" shot may be used from many yards off the green if the lie and turf are playable.

practices a putter shot out of a trap? Or who practices those smart smacks with a putter that roll the ball over level, closely mowed fairway or the collar of a green up close to the hole? Those "Texas wedge" putter strokes are the easiest to learn and to consistently repeat. A slow, smooth stroke with a backswing in proportion to the distance to the hole is all that's needed for the shot.

A
PRECISE
LOOK AT
A PRECISE
TOOL
—THE CLUB

An important part of how to play golf that three of four average golfers never learn is what length is to be expected from each club under normal conditions with favoring wind.

The U. S. G. A. handicap system says that the "theoretical scratch golfer" on whose average ability the association's course ratings are based, should be able to hit a tee shot that will carry at least 200 yards over a level fairway, then probably roll 20 or 25 yards depending on the wind, the condition of turf and slope of fairway. The carry of other wood shots is from 5 to 10 yards, shorter, per number of club. His Number 2 iron shot should carry 180 or 185 yards with reduction of distance of about 10 yards per club until the Number 9 iron will give him about 110 or 115 yards. There often is a difference of 60 yards between the drives of the professional or the strong young amateur and the drive of the 15 handicap player. A playing professional will hit a 5-iron shot 180 yards and the average club member will be doing well if he hits a 5-iron 145 yards.

Often the golfer who watches golf on television is amazed and misled by being told what immense distance stars get out of certain clubs. Newspaper reports of tournament shots also record astounding distances from irons but special conditions such as helping wind, downhill terrain, hard fairways or manipulating the club so a 5-iron virtually becomes a hard-boring 3-iron are significant factors that are not mentioned.

Esquire's authorities remind their pupils to make a habit of pacing off distance after they'd hit what they consider a good average shot with some club and bearing that distance in mind as what could be expected of the club. That advice can be frequently repeated. Most golfers need to heed it.

In his post-mortem of a badly-played hole the ordinary golfer often sees that he was brainless in taking a club that couldn't possibly get him to the green. Then he heaves himself at the ball with the wild hope that he would be able to hit the ball more powerfully than if he had stood up, turned around and whipped the left arm straight, cocked his wrists at the top and uncocked them at the bottom of the swing as he hit down and under the ball. It's the same procedure as any other long shot, except that the player stands a bit closer

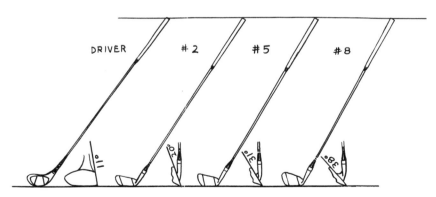

THE LIE OF THE CLUBS
Clubs in a normal set line up across the top like this. As the numbers get higher ball moves in closer to the body and the plane of the swing becomes more upright. You do not need to bend over more to use these shorter clubs unless you choose to shorten up on your grip.

to the ball because the shafts of the longer iron clubs are a little shorter than those of the wood clubs.

THE FACE AND THE LOFT

Most golfers haven't any idea of the loft of faces of clubs and think that a 5-wood, for example, has much more loft than, say, a 3-iron. But the fact is that the 5-wood loft is 21 to 23 degrees in leading manufacturers' lines and the 3-iron has a 23 degree loft; sometimes slightly more.

Iron lofts may vary a degree in different manufacturers' lines but usually run:

Iron Number	2	3	4	5	6	7	8	9	Pitching Wedge	Sand Wedge
Loft (degrees)	20	23	27	31	35	39	43	47	51	58

Wood lofts generally are:

Wood Number	1	2	3	4	5
Loft (degrees)	11	14	17	20	23

The lie of the club varies according to the loft of the clubface and the length of the shaft, with the 62 degree lie and a 36 inch shaft being about medium for the 8-iron and a 54 degree lie with a 42 or 43 inch shaft regarded as standard for a man's driver.

Whether the woods and irons should have standard, flat or upright lies; what flexibility of shaft the clubs should have; the swing weight (the proportion of weight in the head compared to that in the shaft and grip); whether there should be a slight hook or slice built into the assembly of head and shaft; the grip sizes, and other specifications mean more than the average golfer realizes. The experienced professional will spend months and a lot of his own money and bewitch, bother and be-

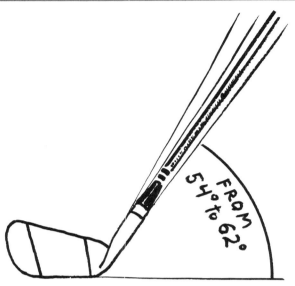

The lie of the club should fit the style of the player.

wilder the head of a manufacturer's club-making staff until the player gets exactly the club that fits him. Yet the ordinary golfer who needs to buy all the help he can get from clubs perfectly suited to his requirements often buys any club that looks like a bargain just because the price is low — and who never hit a good shot with a low-priced club.

When clubs were made by professionals, who knew the swings and the needs of the member who was going to use the club, every club was custom-made. Now, although the matching and gradations of clubs in the inventory of the typical first class country club professional's shop will precisely fit the great majority of the members, the other members need variations from normal that the professional can provide by bench work in the pro shop or by arrangement with manufacturers.

The club member seldom has any idea of how much

study and art there is in fitting clubs. He does not realize that much of the professional's club selling is done on the lesson tee where the professional sees what help the pupil needs and can get from properly fitted clubs.

The golfer himself can watch his fellow member with the toe or the heel of the club off the ground, and see that that particular club is the wrong one for its user.

HOW MUCH SHAFT FLEXIBILITY?

What is needed in shaft flexibility can be determined with certainty only after the expert professional has had an opportunity to make a pretty good analysis of the swing of the club buyer. Generally the stiff shaft is for the strong younger player,the medium shafts for the average male golfer between 35 and 50 years of age and the flexible shaft for the fellow whose muscles are beginning to lose their zip.

Professionals don't dare often say so out loud but they've helped older men by putting women's shafts in the seniors' clubs; the lighter, more flexible women's shafts supply the elasticity the old boys' muscles have lost. Once in a while a defiant senior golfer, unembarrassed, will play with women's clubs and whip the ball around well enough to collect from fellow club members and rate high in state senior tournaments.

Golfers outgrow clubs. The sedentary businessman when he get into his 50s probably doesn't get enough golf to retain what used to be a good swing with good live timing. What he needs in equipment to make up for what he's lost in physical capacity usually has to be determined by an expert's observation and study. His professional may watch him hit a few shots played within eye-range of the pro shop or, much better, observe him during a lesson and learn whether or not different clubs would help him.

Misfit clubs have to be far away from what is needed before the professional will say that they're bad. The pro may be afraid that the pupil may think the professional is trying to "hustle" him to buy a new set of clubs, but the pro wants the member to feel that he comes to the club to enjoy golf, instead of coming out to be the target of a high-powered selling campaign.

At its winter business schools the Professional Golfers Association conducts classes in club fitting. Older professionals pass along what they've learned of this art and science to the progressing younger professionals and assistants. A professional when he goes onto a job at a first class metropolitan district country club has an investment of from $10,000 to $20,000 in golf clubs to supply men and women members. This inventory has to do a comprehensive job of fitting golfers exactly and leave only a small number of cases requiring deviations from a wide range of standard specifications.

If the pro shop stock doesn't provde the correct equipment and if the pro is not competent to fit the member precisely, then the member would take a chance on any cut-price equipment on a catch-as-catch-can basis.

Again the quotable Armour: "The right clubs are the only part of a good golf game you can buy." When Armour was professional at the Boca Raton Club in Florida during winters when it was one of the world's most expensive and exclusive private clubs, then after World War II when it became a resort hotel, he drew distinguished golf enthusiasts from many countries. One was a titled English woman whose secretary had made lesson appointments with Armour months in advance.

She showed at the lesson tee at the time appointed. Armour arose from his comfortable lawn chair under a colorful umbrella and greeted her. He asked her to hit a few shots. He methodically began his lessons with information about the pupil's aptitude and I.Q. Then he would discuss the instruction plan. After that the stroking part of the lesson began.

After seeing this visitor hit the first few shots he asked, "May I see those clubs?" He took a club from her hand and inspected the other equipment in the bag.

Tommy shook his head sadly. "The man who sold you those clubs should have been arrested." Then he sent his assistant into the Boca Raton shop for clubs of correct weights and shafts for his pupil.

The majority of golfers never learn much about their clubs. If golfers weren't usually in a hurry they would benefit greatly by a half-hour discussion and demonstration a competent professional could conduct on why clubs are designed and built the way they are. The experienced professional after showing the ordinary golfer why the sand wedge is designed as it is, can take the pupil into a trap and give him all the basic training he needs on the use of the club in 15 minutes. The finer points the pupil has to learn for himself. That's the way it ought to be done for all practical purposes for the pro isn't going to be at the pupil's side when the shots are to be made in competition.

HOW CLUBS "INFLUENCE" THE SWING

When a putter feels good and rolls the ball in the desired direction no questions are asked. But the expert knows why the putter just happens to fit him. Instinctively the club encourages him to stand in a position where he can keep his body steady and is built so he naturally happens to stroke the ball on the "sweet spot," the center of balance of the clubhead. The expert when he is putting very well is careful and lucky about having his putter soled flat at address and to swing the clubface into contact with the ball when the face is in a square position across the direction line.

It may have been noticed by the studious golfer that the expert who is putting well strikes the ball with the lower end of the shaft always in the same position relative to the ball. John Reuter, Jr., for many years a professional and clubmaker, figured out the design of his Bull's Eye so the "sweet spot" would be below the point where the shaft was joined to the head making it easier to set the club accurately behind the ball. Reuter's design has been the most popular type of putter ever made.

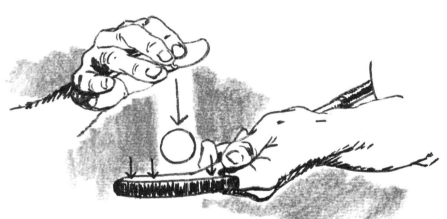

The "sweet spot" of a putter can be precisely located by dropping a ball at various points on the clubface. You will instantly recognize the point of solid rebound.

THE
EXPLOSIVE
CHARGE WITHIN
THE BALL

Fitting the compression of the ball to the player, theoretically, is nearly as important as fitting the club to the player but it just doesn't seem to work out that way because of the psychological factor. The ordinary golfer wants the same high compression in ball winding that the hard-hitting expert gets; 90 to 100. But what makes the golf ball go is the rebound and the high-handicap player simply can't bat the high compression ball hard enough to compress it to its maximum reaction. Furthermore, there aren't many times during a round when the high-handicap player hits the ball in his best possible manner. Some great players after record rounds have said that they felt that they'd hit only six or seven shots perfectly. Even with the average player's incapacity to recognize the feel of a perfectly hit shot, it is probable that he doesn't hit more than four or five of his best shots in one of those rounds when he is respectably under 100.

One golf ball manufacturer says that for the player whose maximum distance is 175 yards a 70 compression ball is most practical; for the fellow who hits up to 225 yards the 80 compression ball is what he should use and for those who drive over 225 yards a 90 or 100 compression ball is to be recommended.

A golf ball is one of the delicate jobs of rubber goods manufacturing yet the ball gets severe pounding and slashing. Cover material and painting of golf balls keep them looking good after actually getting considerable punishment that may have altered the balance of the ball internally, hence affecting its direction and distance.

The United States Golf Association limits the length of the golf ball by ruling that "the velocity of the ball shall not be greater than 250 feet per second when measured on the U.S.G.A. apparatus." Possibly three per cent of all golfers can hit a ball long enough to be concerned about limitation of ball distance.

A
LESSON
IN
BASIC
TRAINING

Some years ago Eddie Loos gave a printed lesson in an article called "The Simple Game Called Golf."

That short bit of pedagogy stirred lively discussion among professionals and ambitious amateurs. Loos then was professional at the wealthy Lake Shore Country Club in northern suburban Chicago. He was a wonder-worker in teaching rich, middle-aged businessmen how to play consistently well. Eddie's members bet high. But most of them played so close to their handicaps there wasn't much won or lost at the end of the season.

Loos was a good player in the early '20s. He finished in the first dozen or so in several National Open championships and won or finished high in lesser tournaments of that period. He resembled the celebrated Leo Diegel of those years. Both young men had nerves that shook them out of competition. They suffered the tortures of the damned with bellyaches during championships. Maybe they had acute attacks of cramps or perhaps they had ulcers, or who knows? But despite their technical excellence neither of them could hold a game together with confidence.

In getting his Esquire lesson started Eddie told that a member of his Club advised him to take care of his club members, and study the teaching of golf so he'd be going good at 50 instead of being through at 30 as a tournament contender.

Loos wrote: *"Golf is simple. It is just one big 'Do' and no 'Don'ts.' And if you follow the 'Do' there are no 'Don'ts.' Today I so instruct my pupils that they think of only one thing. And when they swing, they are thinking as I think — and swinging as I swing as a result.*

"And I'm proud of my pupils. They swing like golfers and they hit the ball sweet and true — not like automatons — or people trying to think of ten things at once."

Loos then told about his experience as a witness in a lawsuit. Observing lawyers making a simple matter seem complicated suggested to him that he and other professionals were doing the same confusing job in golf instruction. He continued:

"Too much instruction — too much placing of hands and feet — too many things to remember during an act which only takes a split second to accomplish — too many words.

"I didn't think of all these things myself when I hit a ball. I couldn't. Why should I expect my pupils to do what I could not and did not do?

"And that started me on the new idea — simplification.

"My first clue came when I read about Ernest Jones in England — back from the wars with his right leg amputed above the knee — and shooting in the seventies on a hard course — with one leg."

"I LET THE CLUB SWING ME"

"The obvious answer was 'balance.' But that didn't satisfy me. I went out in a quiet corner and tried taking full swings standing on one leg. I made a discovery — a big one.

"Just so long as I LET THE CLUB SWING ME, I hit the ball and was in perfect balance without thinking about it.

"The moment I tried to force the action of swinging

148

Cardinal Sin No. 1

A BAD CASE OF GRIP
The duffer who scorns what the golf pros advise,
Resembles this oaf—and ain't his grip nize?

the club, I couldn't keep in balance.

*"And—with some modifications and amplifications
that is all there is to it—let the club swing you—that's the
feeling at any rate."*

Ernest Jones came to the United States and for a
while was professional at the Women's National Country Club at Glen Head, Long Island, a long-gone garden
of golfing Eves. Jones developed a number of champions
among his women pupils. After the Women's National
died he established a tutoring studio in Manhattan.

• Men other than Eddie Loos discovered that the Jones
swinging method worked for them. Jones now has spent
a quarter century in remarkably effective golf schooling.
A Jones former assistant, Angel de La Torre, graduated
from the professional post at Club de Campo in Madrid
then came to the United States. He worked with Loos at

149

Lake Shore then became head professional when illness compelled Eddie to quit. One of the de La Torre sons, Manuel, won numerous collegiate championships then turned professional and is now at the Milwaukee Country Club, having excellent success with the instruction method that his father, Ernest Jones and Eddie Loos employed in teaching golfers whose good games have stood up.

Loos, Jones and de La Torre, Sr., compared notes frequently. The elder de La Torre had his own way of telling the pupils why and how to simply swing the club, but all three teachers reached the same results. You can identify their pupils by looking at the graceful, easy swings.

One place where Jones and Loos differed was the grip.

Cardinal Sin No. 2

TEE IS FOR TENSION
He's a frightening sight as he misses his shots;
His teeth are on edge and his muscles in knots.

Jones advocated an interlocking grip with the thumbs and forefingers sensing the feel of the club and doing the principal job of holding, with the remaining fingers as helpers. Loos, as you will read later, maintained that the grip would take care of itself and would be correct when the golfer felt the clubhead and incorrect when there was no feeling of the swinging and hitting end of the club. Apparently Loos believed in letting the pupil learn by the touch of the fingers just what grip was best for flexibility and control.

Eddie presented his principles and details in what he called a "complimentary lesson."

AN EXPERT'S STEP-BY-STEP GOLF LESSON

"You can take this lesson outdoors or in — anywhere you have room to swing a club. As a matter of fact, I brought one businessman's handicap down from fifteen to four by a few lessons given in his office on Mondays.

Well, you're my pupil.

First of all I'll hit a ball with my driver — and unless I fail to practice what I'm preaching, the apple will travel about two hundred and forty yards or so.

Then I'll ask you: 'Was that ball hit hard?'

Chances are, you'll say, 'Yes'... that opens you for point number one.

I'll tell you, 'That ball was not hit at all — by me. It was in the line of my swinging clubhead — at the bottom — in the natural Speed Area.'

When my club contacted the ball, the speed of the clubhead was so great and the force I exercised so little, that it felt like hitting an egg — no resistance — the ball was gone even before I knew it.

I go through this, because the first thing I want to impress you with is the absence of force and the presence of speed.

The ball is hit by the face of the club—the rest of the clubhead is simply weight to back the face and give you 'feel.'

When I swing a club I start the clubhead—the clubface goes back smoothly and easily and yields to the swinging club—then I let the clubhead swing me.

RHYTHM—NOT FORCE

My mind is on the club*face* when I address the ball— I know where that clubface is—the part which hits the ball—every second—back—down—through and finish. So does every scratch player in the world. Ask any of them if this isn't true.

But—I don't try to control the position of the clubface. I just try to stand and swing so that it comes into proper position at impact *by itself*.

I don't have to watch the ball— I can hit it blindfolded if I stay easy—remember the clubface and let the clubhead swing me.

Now you have the general idea. Speed with rhythm (*not* force) drives the balls—your mind on the clubface—let the clubhead swing you.

AN EXERCISE TO "FEEL" THE CLUBHEAD

Let's see if we can give you the 'feel' of the clubhead.

Take hold of that driver—but—hold it by the *head* instead of the grip.

What do you feel? Nothing, of course, because you are holding the club by the heavy end.

Now take hold properly—by the grip.

What do you feel now?

The clubhead of course. And that is what you must feel—every moment the club is in your hands.

Suppose we try a simple little exercise that will accustom you to 'feeling the clubhead'—and feeling that

152

EXERCISING FOR CLUBHEAD FEEL
An exercise to accustom you to "feeling" the clubhead: hold club
before you and "write" your name with it in the air.

clubhead is one of the few fundamentals of success in golf.

Hold the club in front of you and 'write your name' in the air.

Make it as near vertical writing as you can — this because the major wrist action in golf is up and down — and you might as well acquire the right wrist action at the same time you're working on the feel of the clubhead.

Do that for a while — do it for a long while. That's one reason club makers in the old days used to hit a ball well. They acquired and retained the 'feel of the clubhead' handling clubs in the shop — control became instinctive through continual testing the 'feel' of different clubs they were working on.

Write your name until you feel that the clubhead is writing it for you.

Then you have the feel.

And remember when you stand up to hit the ball — you must feel that clubhead through the whole swing just as you did in writing your name.

Now look out!

I'm going to put you back in kindergarten even if your handicap is six. Take the mashie out of your bag.

Write your name with it for a minute or two so you get the feel.

What's that? You ask if your grip is right? I'm not interested.

Your grip will take care of itself. It's right when you feel the clubhead and wrong when you don't.

Now — still feeling the clubhead — start brushing the grass — skimming it with the club — brush the grass every time you come through — keep it swinging back and forth — that's fine, you're feeling the clubhead and letting it swing you.

This is going to be a little harder.

154

THE GREEN-EYED GOLFER
Lifting the head is a frequent complaint
Which some golfers have and some golfers ain't.

Set the club down as if you were going to hit a ball and then take it back and brush the grass coming through.

You 'lost' the clubhead that time — try it again. Now it's working.

Let's put down a dozen balls — about a foot apart.

Just let the club swing through and take the ball in its path — smooth and easy. Never mind direction. Get used to the clubhead feel.

Put the balls down again. You have the clubhead feel — this time start thinking of the club*face*.

On the next one THINK YOUR LINE TO THE HOLE and swing the clubface through on the line.

Fine. That was straight but too far.

That one was better but short.

This time think *both* line *and* distance.

Perfect — in short shots you think *both* line and distance. In full shots you think *only* the line.

SETTING THE STANCE

Be easy and comfortable. If you think the line when you address and let the clubhead swing you with your mind on the club*face*, you'll subconsciously adjust your stance to the direction you're thinking.

Ah — that sounds complicated, doesn't it?

Well — it isn't. But that's why I want you to keep at these short shots a while. After all, these short shots are the Speed Area of the big shots — the only difference is that they're a segment instead of the full circle.

And, after you have worked on short shots, after you demonstrate you can THINK THE LINE AND DISTANCE and let the CLUBHEAD SWING YOU knowing always where the FACE is — then and not before, I'll try to start you on half shots — but you'll rebel and insist on the driver and against my will, I'll give in. After all, you've been pretty patient.

156

START SWING FROM THE INSIDE

All right — you have the driver in your hand.

In these full shots you want to swing your circle through the back of the ball — therefore you start your swing toward the inside — back and around — and the moment inertia is overcome and you begin to feel the head swinging — the club swings you — and travels around — finds its own path in back of you and up between your neck and your right shoulder at the top.

You don't have to think about starting it down — or breaking your wrists or straightening them — all those things are automatic so long as you feel that clubhead just as you did in writing your name.

Just keep your head as the hub of the wheel — stay easy — and — the ball is an incident in the path of the clubhead.

Cardinal Sin No. 4

SUPERSONIC SWING
MacMayhem's swing has such terrible force
He misses the ball as a matter of golf course.

Now there were two reasons why I kept you at the short pitches – apart from the fact that they are important in scoring.

The first reason was to get you thinking the direction by continuous concentration on the clubface.

The second reason was even more important if such a thing is possible.

Here it is:

The bottom of the swing is the Speed Area when the swing is being made.

But in starting the swing – in taking the club away from the ball – it is the INERTIA segment.

In other words, the club addressing the ball is in a state of INERTIA which must be overcome to start the club swinging away.

This is where ninety-nine per cent of the players go wrong – if the swing is improperly started at this point it will never right itself.

You must overcome the inertia – start your full swing with the same delicacy and control you would use in a twenty-foot pitch to the green.

'Slow back' won't do it. You can lose the clubhead in a slow start as well as a fast one.

Overcome that inertia delicately – smoothly – feel the flow of the clubhead start – feel it almost at once – no pressure – just play the clubhead for the start of a two-hundred yard drive or a half buried iron shot just as you would the mashie pitch to the green – lots of smoothness, not effort, does the work.

This is the vital part – the start of the swing – when I get off on my long shots, I go back to short pitches to regain the 'clubhead feel.'

Perhaps I can describe it this way – the first few feet – the lower segment of the swing gets the 'feel of the clubhead' in your fingers and hands – from that point on—THE CLUB SWINGS YOU.

Get the feel in the first few feet—then—let the club-head swing you. Let it swing you back—let it swing you through.

The ball is an incident—it happens to be in the way of the clubface which is the one thing you are conscious of throughout the swing.

You're accustomed to driving two hundred yards. All right.

For the time being, I don't want you to try to drive over a hundred and fifty or a hundred and sixty at most—but let the clubhead swing you. Think of the face and direction.

Now swing it.

What's that? Certainly the ball went two hundred yards at least. That's an object lesson in *not hitting*.

THE DIFFERENCE BETWEEN IRONS AND WOODS

To me there is only one difference and that is in the length of the shaft which of itself determines the angle of the swing.

There is no difference in the playing. Unless I am buried, I take no turf with irons—make no attempt to hit them.

And my iron shots go as far and true as the next fellow's.

Some of you are going to quarrel with the utter lack of instruction for stance—address—pivot and all the other time honored fetishes of conventional golf instruction.

Deeds speak louder than words—and somebody else's deeds perhaps show less bias than mine might. For example, I refer you to my memory of Ernest Jones himself *sitting on a chair—and hitting a ball two hundred yards!*

My next memory picture is of my old friend Leo Diegel hitting his shot *standing on one foot*—he has

UNBALANCED BEHAVIOR
With unbalanced stance in addressing the ball
The address is unknown — if he hits it at all.

scored in the 70's standing on his right foot alone. What price stance, pivot, etc.?

Well, I have certainly succeeded in using a lot more words than I expected to. But, after all, I've just been saying the same thing over and over again. And that's golf — doing the right thing over and over again so that it becomes muscular memory.

It takes a deal of patience to get this idea into your muscles.

But there's one grand thing about it. It stays. Once there, your 'off days' will be few and far between.

And — when you do get off — back to the short pitches — to remind you.

So — that's the end of the lesson. The rest of it is up to you."

ETIQUETTE
OR
HOW GOLFERS
ACT LIKE
HUMANS

Golf is the only game having its etiquette codified in 12 articles of conduct representing several centuries of civilized experience.

The Rules of Golf begin with "Section 1 — Etiquette."

This initiation to a formal career as a golfer is not merely an old-fashioned matter of good manners. The section on Etiquette presents an ingenious balance of privileges, responsibilities and procedures which, when observed, contribute greatly to the enjoyment of the game by gentleman or heel, lady or hag.

Unfortunately, although the section on Etiquette is very simple it is somewhat like the words of the second verse of the national anthem, good stuff but read by practically nobody. However, the Ten Commandments also haven't been read by millions of decent people who instinctively observe the Decalogue. The Gentleman Sportsman who goes by the Golden Rule doesn't find himself out of bounds anywhere.

Golf's code of etiquette is much more accurate than handwriting, astrology or palmistry in revealing character. Most of the performances required as golfing good manners come naturally to the socially educated man, woman or child. A few items of the written or unwritten code of etiquette are technical matters that essentially involve consideration for other golfers and shouldn't call for much more than simple reminders.

161

"Stop saying it's just a game—it's *not* just a game!"

In the category of details that suggest that you give mind to the other golfer (who sometimes may be you) are smoothing footprints in sandtraps, keeping bag carts and golf cars off areas where their traffic wears turf unduly thus deteriorating playing conditions, replacing divots, and slowing play to a tiresome gait.

THE GROUND RULES START WITH THE GROUND

Replacement of divots no longer is an item of good conduct at some courses. When divots are chopped out at these courses maintenance procedure is to repair the scars with soil, seed and fertilizer. With fairway watering and warm sunshine, the repair is completed quickly. In Japan, girl caddies carry small bags containing a soil, seed and fertilizer mixture which they promptly apply to divots.

When you neglect to smooth your tracks in a trap, the next fellow may knock a shot into the bunker and have it come to rest in a heel print that he heatedly identifies as a handicap, unmistakably left by a heel in more ways than one. Regardless of what's said about the wedge making shots out of sand easy, playing a ball lying in a solidly packed heel print or on a sandy ledge left when some thoughtless person climbed up the steep bank of a trap instead of walking out by the low side, is a tough shot for the best of them as well as a needless difficulty. The fellow who has to play shots from such lies ought to realize that he also might be a transgressor who sins against those who follow him.

Ring Lardner, who got a lot of fun out of playing a great deal of bad golf, once taught band leader Paul Whiteman a tactful lesson in golf manners. Whiteman at that time must have weighed over 250 pounds. He was a graceful fat guy and a pretty fair golfer. Lardner wrote a funny piece on playing hard shots in golf in which he said that the most miserable shot in the game was one out of a Whiteman footprint. After that citation Whiteman became a model of etiquette in taking a trap rake or a club and making the trap so smooth you practically could shoot pool on it. Or if Whiteman didn't do the job personally he would stay behind to supervise his caddy as he did it for him.

Possibly the most violated rule of golf is the rule prohibiting grounding of a club in a sand trap. The reason for this rule is to maintain the character of the trap as a hazard and a punishment. When a club is grounded behind a ball in the sand the effect is to tee up the ball and actually make the shot easier instead of harder as it should be on account of the previous shot having missed the target.

Usually there is simple equity in the rules of golf, protecting as well as punishing those who play by the rules. Actually that is the only way that golf can be played for if you're not playing by the rules you are not playing golf.

There always will be debates about what is and what is not good sense and justice about some rules of golf. For instance, the addition of a penalty stroke for a ball hit out of bounds is declared by some to be an illogical penalty because the player would have been better off to miss the ball altogether.

Differences of opinion between the United States Golf Association representing millions of club members and unattached amateurs and, on the other side, the Professional Golfers Association were settled. So, in 1964, began the first year of uniform rules the United States has had in quite a while. During the discussion that ended with the agreement, amateur fun golfers declared that they were playing by rules more severe than experts playing for money. The propaganda aspect of the situa-

"It doesn't make any difference *which* club you use here"

tion didn't glorify the stars who were expected to be masters of all the niceties of technique. Practically, the differences didn't amount to much. Hence the tournament professionals had nothing to lose and higher prestige to gain by playing the same rules as the amateur.

The male golfer, professional or amateur, generally is more vocal in expressing his pain at the severity of a course or a ruling than is the lady contestant. It is not at all unusual for a club's women golfers to know the rules better than the men members do, hence to know and expect penalties for violations. At many clubs the women's committee starts its year's program with rules, explanations and discussions at which the club's professional or experienced women golfers are the instructors.

A customary excuse for ignorance of golf's rules is that they're too long and too complicated. As a matter of fact, though, the Rules of Golf are shorter than the rules of baseball and the collegiate or professional football rules. This may be surprising, considering that baseball and football are played on grounds of uniform dimensions and no two golf courses are alike.

The design of the golf course may have a player out of sight of his opponent and in position to accidentally or deliberately break the law of the game and unfairly benefit from an unobserved violation of the rules.

In instances of unseen infractions of the code the violator is expected to announce the violation. There have been so many cases of unobserved breaches in important competitions being declared and the penalty accepted with pain, but without protest, that the subject long ago ceased to be sports section news.

The obligation of a golfer calling a penalty on himself bewildered the gorillas whose prohibition affluence got them into golf, as a symbol of social improvement or as a balance for boyhood spent in drab and dreary en-

"He never misses—since he got that 'radio beam' idea"

vironment or because of some other impulse. Several of the hoodlums became quite good golfers. One of them, a party having the *nom de trigger* of Machinegun Jack McGurn, became competent to the degree that he could qualify for sectional amateur championships.

The hoodlums' amazement was boundless when they were informed that the game they were playing required that they snitch on themselves and were told that not knowing the rules wasn't an alibi for cheating. There wasn't honor among bootleggers any more than there is among other thieves, regardless of folklore, but pastiming mobsters of the prohibition era were remarkably frank in announcing such not uncommon penalizing accidents as a club hitting the ball twice on shots out of a sand trap or a ball moving after address.

There were sizable bets on many of these games so the mystery of the power of golf law in these incidents of self-proclaimed law-breaking by prohibition's golfing gentry, baffled and sometimes embarrassed reputable citizens who for various reasons or none — happened to be playing with the mobsters.

It has been estimated that a golfer's chances of making a hole-in-one are much greater than the probability that he will read the rules of the game. That's regrettable because the rules really are interesting. They provide good entertainment in club grill-room replays of rounds as well as adding to the golfers' education during the play.

FIRST GOLF IS FOR PLAYERS NOT SPECTATORS

When the golfer begins his education in playing the game as it should be played he promptly is informed by Article 1, Section 1, of the preamble on Etiquette that golf is fundamentally a participant's game; not a spectacle. That is the nature of the game and anyone who doesn't go along with the idea doesn't have a gun drawn on him to make him join in the play. He can come in or stay out. Golf has stood the test of centuries and does not appear to be in urgent need of drastic changes.

Generally galleries at golf tournaments are remarkably well behaved. There is a belief that the considerate department of golf tournament galleries has made tournament players unduly sensitive to actual or imagined disturbances. Those who hold this opinion declare that for the money the tournament star wins he ought to be able to concentrate, like Willie Mays or the late George Herman Ruth, on hitting the ball instead of worrying about a camera being clicked at him. Those who pay to get into a golf tourney and gallop around a course for

168

intermittent views of the contestants in action are inclined to think that the etiquette of golf also calls for tournament players giving the paying customers respectful consideration. When a tournament spectator looks at a golf tournament program and sees in it 24 "Tips to Gallery" he may wonder how many "Tips to Players" are issued by the Professional Golfers Association to make certain that there is an equalization of etiquette between the players and the gallery from whom fiscal and publicity blessings flow.

It must be said for the players that, considering any mortal's eagerness to be able to blame his mistakes on somebody else and the numerous opportunities afforded in tournament golf to make honest use of a good alibi, the tourney star's nerve and deportment control are above normal.

Keen observers at golf tournaments have commented that complaints of gallery misbehavior almost always are made by players who aren't playing too well or, to put it charitably, aren't getting lucky bounces. Possibly the accurate and kindly way of looking at the tournament golfer's self-control (or lack of it) is from the viewpoint of Lincoln Werden, the New York Times' noted golf authority. Werden, commenting on a petulant performance by a famous professional, said "When he's going good, nothing bothers him; when he is going bad everything upsets him."

THE CREED OF SILENCE

Incidents that amuse, bewilder or disgust tournament spectators involve the use of cameras. Professionals who make excellent steady-nerved shots when they are playing highly paid exhibitions while television cameras are whirring, and photographers and other technicians are in action, get disturbed and irate when newspaper photographers shoot pictures after the pro stars have hit their shots. Even the aiming of a camera will upset some professionals.

Newspaper photographers usually are golfers. They are as aware of the etiquette of the golf photographing situation as the professionals and (so the photographers declare) as competent in their demanding, often dangerous and never overpaid profession as the golf professionals are in their own work. Hence the photographers maintain that the golf professional or amateur who says that a newspaper or magazine photographer has ruined a golf shot is a man or woman trying to pass the buck in a manner unbecoming a genuine champion.

In fairness to the professional golfers, male or female, it must be said that the inconsiderate amateur photographer who smuggles a still or motion picture camera into a golf gallery can and does shatter the traditional silence of a golf gallery by ill-timed click or rataplan and jerk at the nerves of a shotmaking contestant. As rare as these cases are there are just enough of them to make professional golfers apprehensive. It is an unfortunate situation peculiar to golf. Although newspaper sports photographers and golf writers can't think of a tournament golf shot definitely spoiled by bad timing of a newspaper cameraman, the controversy certainly has reduced the quantity and quality of first class action photographs of pro golfers and has golf, pictorially, running nearly last on sports pages.

Innocently or deliberately some golfers have disturbing personalities or mannerisms that must be regarded as an unwelcome but interesting part of the game. These unpleasant features are tests to which golf occasionally subjects its devotees.

In match play psychological warfare, when within the broad boundaries of gamesmanship, is regarded as part of the game although the practice of encouraging the other guy to beat himself has diminished from the crest of genius it reached during the colorful match play years of the PGA championship. Walter Hagen could conduct a war of nerves with serene and supreme skill. Tommy Armour and Gene Sarazen also were brilliantly talented.

In the lore of the professionals' American championships the final of the 1930 PGA in which Armour defeated Sarazen 1 up shines as an exhibit of a head-on clash between two master needleworkers. Sarazen normally was rather a fast player and Armour usually was a slow operator. But in the final round Armour opened the throttle and played faster than Sarazen. The shrewd Sarazen sensing his opponent's tactics slowed down until he played slower than Armour ever had.

Psychological warfare which once was a feature of the personality clashes of match play now has nearly gone out of fashion in the male National Amateur and Intercollegiate championships, but you may see sparkles of this competitive factor in the Senior male championships. Once in a while the girls in their major amateur championships will dart a claw out deftly but never is there enough of this to make the competition a cat show.

There are experienced observers of tournament golf who believe that the educational value of match play's inevitable war of nerves is reflected in the tactics of Jack Nicklaus who has had more tough match play experience than any other of the present roster of pro stars and who got that training not too long ago. When Nicklaus meets Palmer, Player or any of the other ranking experts in play-offs or comes down the stretch paired with them the match play schooling gives Nicklaus the advantage, according to numerous golf writers. The good record Nicklaus has in the play-offs and final rounds seems to confirm the experts' opinion.

To what extent the needle is a weapon of honorable golfing warfare probably depends on temperament rather than ethics. To some golfers part of the fun of the game is getting the opponent uneasy even if there's very little money or none at all involved. Money in an amateur golf competition is a comparative factor. What is only a casual wager to rich gamblers playing at winter golfing vacation courses may be a gigantic amount to other golfers.

"Hustling" is a department of semi-pro golf which consists in luring the unwary and avaricious into play that is not competition if the hustler can prevent any uncertainty. Southeastern Florida in the winter and the Los Angeles area throughout the year long have been major centers of the golf hustling traffic with the New York metropolitan district a poor third and the Chicago territory a distant fourth. Las Vegas, where gambling on golf tournaments has apprehensive golfers fearful of a scandal, experiences very little golf hustling. Seemingly those Las Vegas citizens and visitors who are most agreeable to gambling sizeable amounts are wary in appraising the competitors, the competition and the odds in golf.

THE INTRICACIES OF THE HANDICAP SYSTEM

The handicapping systems in golf which theoretically and to a large extent, practically, provide fair and close competition have been carefully worked out to eliminate or at least minimize hustling at private clubs where members turn in their scores after each round played as the basis for handicaps. Course ratings also figure in the determination of handicaps as a score consistently made on an easy course would not indicate the player's ability on a more difficult course.

Handicaps are revised monthly during the playing season at most private clubs, in accordance with the practice of the district golf association of which the club is a member, or by the United States Golf Association recommendation which has a handicap system based on the best 10 of a player's last 25 scores, compared with the course rating.

In some areas no scores higher than two strokes over par are considered in computing handicaps; the belief being that a person planning larceny might deliberately toss away a lot of strokes on the last few holes in order to establish a handicap higher than deserved. The noble effort, to better the record of the Commandments telling the golfer not to covet thy neighbor's goods and not to steal, possibly has been somewhat successful. But there is a not impious conviction that the screening of club membership committees and the suspicion and scorn of honest club members has chiefly protected the value of the handicap system against the forces of darkness and evil.

The Calloway system of handicapping, invented by an ingenious veteran professional, takes good care of golfers who are playing without formal handicaps in such competitions as trade organization events.

Tom MacMahon, who has given considerable time and effort determining an equitable handicap system, cheerfully admits that the popular practice of conceding putts makes any handicap system used at a club only a polite, though close, guess. MacMahon has seen so many putts of less than 2 feet missed that he maintains that no stroke play scorecard can be regarded as accurate unless every putt has been holed. There have been putts of 6 inches missed in national championships when players, taking careless taps, hit into the green and never touched the ball.

A putt that is easy in practice becomes terribly difficult when there is a slight element of nervous tension yipping at the muscles. Nobody knows that any better than the practical, mercenary psychologist, the golf hustler. If you have watched a hustler operate, either as a captive or as a fortunate observer who can't be burned, you possibly have noticed that, magnanimously, the hustler will allow his prey a Mulligan off the tee now and then but will concede a putt rarely and only for tactical purposes.

(Incidentally the origin of the term Mulligan, meaning a second drive after the first one is unsatisfactory, never has been established.)

Match play strategy often has opponents conceding fairly long putts early in the competition, each fellow trusting that the other will lose the feel for the shorter putts that will have to be made when the match is close and nearing the end.

THE POLITE PACE OF THE GAME

Reference has been made to the pace of play as a tactical factor in match play. It also can be an influence in medal play for when a player who normally is rather fast is paired with a player who is slow both, subconsciously, may have their timing affected. Pace of play is a curious and expensive matter. Slow play of professionals on television, especially in preparing for putting, has been imitated by so many rank and file golfers that the common time of an 18-hole round has been increased from the three hours of the '20s and early '30s to today's time of about four hours, often even more. This slow-down has had the effect of reducing course capacity and probably has many believing they haven't got the time for golf.

At public courses, course rangers speed up dilatory players. In the United States Golf Association's National Open championship, the top event in tournament golf, contestants are warned that they'd better get moving or they'll be penalized. At private clubs usually the rule, printed or tacit, is that if there is a hole open ahead of any foursome that foursome must allow golfers following them to play through. In recent years the rule has been underlined by letters of rebuke from club committees to notoriously and persistently slow players. The embarrassment and acrimonious discussion at least has made all club members conscious of the responsibility

"He's the club's bottleneck"

to keep from delaying players after them.

Use of the golf car hasn't made the game faster. Often the car must go from side to side of a fairway carrying clubs of the two riders and must be parked at one side of a green while putters or sand wedges are in use. Car time probably will be reduced during a round as players get better educated in where and how to drive.

The big loss of time is on the greens where dilatory procedure becomes a habit. There is no reason for taking much time in determining a line from the ball to the hole when such a line changes direction a couple of times due to the contour of the green. Psychologists say that such a route is guessed more accurately by relying on conditioned subconsciousness rather than straining at the job in an effort to be mechanical. They also remark that standing over the ball too long before putting probably increases tension instead of easing it.

What the sensible pace is for the individual golfer nobody can tell. Julius Boros, with the laziest-looking backswing of all golf's stars, doesn't waste a moment or a movement in putting when he is putting well. Arnold Palmer is one of the best putters modern golf has seen, but when his putting slumps observers believe that he's taking more than his normal time in lining up and stroking the putt.

Complaints about slow players are not a new development in golf. There always have been a few tournament golfers who take abnormally long in shotmaking and of these only two or three have been unusually good. No player has been penalized for slow play in the National Open, the Masters or the Professional Golfers Association championship although several have been warned to come alive and get going in the National Open.

No warning seems to have hurt the game of the offending player, but, to the contrary, each admonition has been followed by sharp scoring thus giving reason for the hunch that at least one famous player might have added to his string of championships had he played fast enough to keep ahead of his worrying.

There are amusing aspects of the slow play problem. At the Masters for years the oldest players in the field, Fred McLeod and Jock Hutchison, were the first to tee off. McLeod had won the National Open in 1908. Hutchison's first big win was the PGA of 1920. These patriarchs, well into their 70s, would go up and down the hills of the Augusta National course faster than any of the younger players, finish their round with respectable socres and be enjoying their sips of Scotch in the clubhouse while the fresher talent was still out on the course trailing far behind the agile and ancient athletes.

The slow player was a nuisance to be considered in 1858 in the championship at St. Andrews which blossomed into the British Open. The field of 28 included Robert Chambers, 20, the youngest player in the field and D. Wallace, in his 60s and the oldest competitor. Wallace was a maddeningly slow player. Dr. J. G. Macpherson wrote: "Old Wallace would have carried the championship at the final tussle of the tournament by his wearisome style, had not Robert Chambers' temper been particularly easygoing. 'Give me a novel and a campstool and I'll let the old chap do as he likes', was his remark when pitted against the slowpoke."

Chambers was the winner. He became a famous publisher, but of his golf after defeat of the slow-moving Wallace the record books say naught.

Whenever there is anything written about golf manners a tendency is to attribute violations of the code of etiquette to the pay-as-you-play golfers and envision the private club member as a *veray parfit gentil knight* who, because of his virtues has merited the Supreme Court and constitutional grant of being allowed to herd with his kind. The truth is that among the club member's virtues is not always that of maintaining a reasonable pace at play. The public course player has to keep moving sensibly or is asked to get off or, more emphatically, reminded to be considerate when some big strong guy in a traffic jam behind him lets a shot fly into him.

The slow playing club member makes necessary starting times on Saturdays, Sundays and holidays at a number of private clubs, hence, in one respect, puts his club even with the public course.

This trouble of slow play has been emphasized by the popularity of the game and the crowded condition of many courses. It also has spotlighted the personalities of members whose admission to excellent private clubs has been questioned by fellow members stalled behind the slow-movers.

THE BUSINESS OF BEING A CLUB MEMBER

Although qualifications for membership at such moments of aggravation are not a subject for judicial deliberation, there are occasional comments that mistakes are made by membership committees who have the responsibility for screening applicants for membership so only gentlemen sportsmen and their congenial families will be admitted to the club.

Due to lack of information a candidate may be admitted to club membership because he is financially, rather than socially, desirable but when in the club he may spend so little and that so reluctantly he doesn't do the club a bit of good.

Often a young husband who has payments on a mortgage, children to clothe, feed and send through school and a beautiful young wife faithful and full of frolic, shies away from club membership where he and his family would contribute more to the Club's prestige and pay a much bigger share of the club operating expenses than a rich old guy would.

However, there is the accompanying fact that many younger people graduate into private club membership without having the slightest notion that such membership is a privilege that involves responsibilities.

A private golf club doesn't pay its operating costs with social status. Everybody has to pay cash in carrying a share of the financial load.

Generally, the country club's food is of highest quality, fairly well prepared and served by a staff that is inactive 80 per cent of the working week.

"I'm afraid it was a mistake having the runner-up present the cup"

The expense of maintaining the golf course in the condition demanded by members of a first class metropolitan district private club is from $3 to $9 per round.

The professional at a private club usually is paid only a nominal salary. His other assured income commonly includes what he can net out of club storage and cleaning and in numerous cases all or part of the revenue of golf car rental.

His main source of income is from selling merchandise in the pro shop and from giving golf instruction. So, what the pro job amounts to is giving the professional a chance to make a living that is good enough to warrant a good man giving good service to qualified members of a good club. It seems to be a sound arrangement, as with few exceptions, the clubs that are most desirable from a membership viewpoint have the most competent professionals.

The pro shop primarily is for the convenience of the golfer. The pro shop idea was born when professionals made clubs and balls along the more popular Scotch courses. The pro shop grew to be one of the big businesses in sports when American golfers discovered how useful a well run pro shop could be to each club and its members.

When the golfers learned that what's good for the club's professional is good for the club and all its members the golf boom got going strong. The first class professional has proved to be a tremendously effective promoter of golf interest and play not only among the men, women and children at his club, or at the pay-as-you-go course at which he is employed, but in taking the gospel into schools.

Logically then, support of the professional's efforts became a recognized obligation of the private club member just as the member is expected to share in the cost of the superior and restricted services of the club's restaurants, bars, swimming pool and other facilities. The policy has worked out very well for all concerned as the patron of the pro shop gets the top grades of golf merchandise, many of the products being made exclusively for the professionals' customers.

Club officials admit, with embarrassment, that there often is a need for education of club members. The member is assumed to know that when he is elected to membership he has the responsibility of sharing in the costs as well as in the privileges of club operation. He commonly is aware that it is a breach of good manners and club business requirements to bring his own bottle of Old Burn Belly into the grill room, but doesn't realize that he also is supposed to patronize his club's professional department even if it may cost him $20 a year more than cut-price buying.

There are certain obligations of consideration for condition of the course and for regulations involving operation of the clubhouse and other facilities. The club rules and by-laws, of course, rarely are read but there really isn't any need to pour over them as they merely put into print what any person having the happy combination of social intelligence and stable economic status knows inherently.

Due to the rapid development of the Great Society in the United States there are members of country clubs who haven't reached the stage of being educated to their obligations as members of an organization for mutual enjoyment and responsibilities. Ostensibly these people are desirable club members or they'd not have passed screening of the membership committee if the club is what it professes to be.

Probably the great majority of the members ignorant of their obligations are potentially ideal members, but

"May we play through?"

the job of educating them is a delicate one that nobody wants. Hence it is common to see that about 70 per cent of a club's operating revenue comes from about 30 per cent of the members, frequently because some members never have appreciated that belonging to a club calls for spending one's share of the money club operation requires.

Some members are stretched thin financially and may be in over their heads as club members, but those cases actually are rare despite the high cost of club membership.

The costs of membership in the better metropolitan district country clubs are so high, due to heavy fixed and operating charges, that there is a deplorable tendency to prevent desirable people from joining. Among those exceptionally good ones are, as has been mentioned, young men who are progressing rapidly in business

"Well, it used to be out in the country"

and who have attractive, socially poised wives and, with the population explosion, and mortgages, have costs prior to those involved in country club membership. Luckily, expense accounts often help. A bright young man pleasantly operating at a golf club on a potential customer is a substantial economic asset to the nation and the sort of individual who pays a goodly percentage of the tax collectors' salaries as well as other ransom to Washington. That may be one of the reasons for a slight — but very slight — easing of a discriminatory tax burden on country clubs.

GOLF
AND
TOURISM

A conspicuous development of the golf picture is in its relationship to travel. Golf has given new impetus to tourism. Reduction of import allowances and high prices abroad have reduced the American woman's interest in shopping which used to be her big game overseas, but now that she has found she can play golf with her husband in foreign lands a new area of delight has been opened.

Hawaii now has a few of the finest courses in the United States. Mexico, where land of golf course character is not abundant, has some exceptionally good new courses due to the foresight of the government's tourism department and a veteran golfer, Percy Clifford. France and Italy have excellent new courses as features of housing developments and a half-dozen pretty good older courses. Germany has several really good courses in condition that owes considerable to the interest of the U. S. Military. The course, waters and baths at Baden-Baden will trim down your belly, improve your wind and legs and supplement your wife's beauty parlor treatments—an item of travel expense in which the Germans star.

Spain is coming along fast with golf courses. Along the Mediterranean a few courses have been built that are fascinating; one of them being a Robert Trent Jones display of genius that is the Mare Nostrum version of Pebble Beach. On Majorca the chief hotel man of Spain has had a course built convenient to a hotel established in a former castle. It's an attractive course too, and keeps time pleasantly engaged while the tourist is not vacationing at sleeping, reading, swimming, getting drunk in an enthusiastic and refined sort of a way, watching a bullfight or passing the obedience test as one's wife is shopping.

Scotland, England and Wales have the most beguiling array of courses, ranging from the sublime to the stinking, that any American could hope to see. Even though the American golfing tourist may be a fellow who plays with a strong back and a weak mind he never will forget the distinction of famous holes of the noted Scotch, English and Welsh courses.

The Holy Land of the Old Course at St. Andrews has hidden bunkers, sort of shell hole depressions in fairways, two fairways crossing each other, parallel fairways and double greens on several levels and with trick contours and areas about the size of Rhode Island; gull feathers and manure in which you can lose a ball, and would drive the Green Committee of an American club raving mad, yet is the world's most fascinating golf course.

The first time Bob Jones played St. Andrews in competition he put the ball in his pocket before finishing the round. Hagen finished last in his debut at St. Andrews. Both thought the course was the world's worst. Jones, then a bold, candid young man, said so.

Then they learned to play golf courses and with the knowledge came the awakening. They say how the Old Course had outsmarted them.

Experienced golfers, the canny old pros and cunning senior amateurs who have been around plenty are amused by criticisms of St. Andrews by American golfers—good, medium or bad—who play it only a few times. The criticism of the star pros who are new to

St. Andrews usually is that of fellows who can play golf shots well but who haven't learned what needs to be learned about playing golf courses.

There are four or five courses in South America that are well worth the American golfer's time. Australia has quite a few of them, about a dozen and most of them around Melbourne and Sydney, that will give you testing and entertaining golf. Golf course condition is pretty good there on the larger courses, and on the smaller courses you will play interesting holes in which Allah made up in golf architecture what he forgot in providing greens and fairways of the type you play in the United States.

Very seldom will you get elsewhere fairways and greens of the quality you get in the United States. At Gleneagles' two courses in Scotland, a British railroads resort, the greens and fairways are as near to the American quality as you'll probably ever see for some years.

Japan has eight or ten surprisingly fine courses and in excellent condition. The fairways, especially, are to the average American club members' liking and the greens, if somewhat slower than American greens, are true. The Japanese girl caddies, a sturdy, extremely competent and cheerful bunch, will contribute to your education and entertainment as a golfer.

You've got to play one of the Hong Kong courses and the Royal Calcutta's new Tollygunge course; the sure-enough championship course with marvelous clubhouse service that you'll find at Taipei, Taiwan, and three courses in the Philippines that are about as exciting as you'll find in most countries. In the Orient you can play at least nine holes that have some reason to be considered among the great golf holes in the world.

Canada is so much like the United States you don't regard playing their courses as touring. In the Canadian

Rockies there are two scenic courses you'll long remember. The Royal Montreal not only is the oldest golf club on this continent but has, in its new course, six or seven of the best golf holes you ever saw. South Africa in a lot of ways is like Canada, and the American golfer there will play with South Africans on very pleasant courses and forget, when he is in the clubhouse, he's more than a few miles from home. The South African professionals Bobby Locke, Gary Player and others found the United States a better deal than the Kimberly diamond mines. They played well and behaved themselves in the Land of the Free and attained a high altitude of solvency.

Puerto Rico, Jamaica, Bermuda and other isles of the Carib have lovely golf courses and if you've got money enough you are daft (the Scots' word for nutty) to buck the blizzards of winter in the United States when you might be playing golf, getting tranquilly alcoholic and sleeping late at balmy spots in the Spanish Main.

Even tiny Israel has succumbed. And in the northland of that tiny country there is a lovely, suprisingly verdant, full sized course. The consistent gag there suggests that Palmer or Nicklaus stay home; one big blast off the tee from those strong boys and the pellet lands in Arab territory.

You can't hardly go any place in the civilized world now without having fine golf available. Air France and the French tourism organization are having a remarkably good course built on Tahiti and anyone who has seen pictures of the romantic Tahitian bunkering knows that playing in that country is a nice investment of time.

Nations' tourism boards extend beguiling invitations to golfers. The British tourist outfit does the best job of this sort for the simple reasons that the British have the most charming golf courses to exhibit in the home-

188

land of the game and because British golfers are no worse than being tied as the most pleasant of all golfing hosts. There are exceptions, of course, as the British also can tie us in having a few club members by whom the great majority are embarrassed. The Germans used to say that the British by bad manners brought on two world wars but very few American golfers ever would damn the British for lacking in graciousness. An American who shows decent manners and knowledge of the sort of protocol he would expect from a British visitor to his own club never has any difficulty in making arrangements to play with a member of a good British club. In fact, the British are far more hospitable to overseas golfers than we are. They usually roll out the red carpet of welcome once, but if the visitor hasn't the grace to fit into the picture there will be a great many tactful and positive reasons found to keep him off the lot the next time. Then, regardless of what he thinks or says about the British, they will be highly pleased by his absence.

There is no more reason for a British private club receiving an American visitor from overseas than there is for an American private club to extend a hearty welcome to a visitor from an out-of-state club. But the British private clubs do have a nice way of making it easy for the socially desirable foreign visitor to play the course once. Then if the visitor who actually is no bargain socially exhibits his lack of manners he is through forever and ever, and ruins the situation for other American visitors for months.

The last great frontier of golf, which some hesitate to mention because of the fear so many will be stampeding toward it that it will be ruined, is Ireland. From the magnificent Royal Portrush in Antrim, a beautiful country of lefthanded infidels (and may their shots drop in

Satan's heel prints); through the blessed shores of Portmarnock, to the tranquil pastures of Mulliger (where you bounce shots off sheep onto the pastoral greens and add your score as you contentedly drink with the community's chief law officer), Ireland can claim to be heaven for the wandering American golfer as it is heaven to the tender kitchen or saloon singer because his mother came from there.

Green committees of American golf courses might want to change about eight out of ten holes on Irish golf courses to their own scheme of things, but the changes would be for dull although perhaps theoretically better golf. Golf courses can be so fancy and smoothly groomed that they become boring. The American golfer learns that as he plays around the world.

HOW
GOLF
GREW
UP

There may be golfers who love to lie before the fire reading history books and kicking their little toes into the floor in excitement but we have never met them.

Everybody who reads the first thing in the chronicle of golf is told that in 1457 Scottish politicians prohibited golf because it interfered with the practice of archery necessary to protect the politicians' job. A half century later, the game was restricted because it was strong competition for sermons. Still later the game was officially interdicted because it was instrumental in sending money out of Scotland into the Netherlands for golf balls.

Nobody seems to have paid much attention to these cease and desist orders against golf. Few have paid much money for history books in which they could read about this prohibitory legislation or other vestigial showings of golf.

Possibly that has been no serious loss except to the ink-stained wretches who write the books in hope of some fame and more fortune but were lucky to reclaim the eating money they spent while in the white heat of research and creation. It should be said, though, that golf has received more scholarly attention than most sports despite the absence of a lot of high class competition in this literary sector.

Golf certainly benefited from being a pastime at St. Andrews, one of the few early outposts of literacy. Tradition declares that in the eighth century, relics of St.

Scots migrating to other lands became widespread missionaries for the game

Andrew were brought by St. Regulus, Bishop of Patras in Achaea, and treasured in a monastery in Scotland on a rock above the North Sea. In 747 St. Andrew became the patron saint of Scotland.

The great University of St. Andrews was chartered in 1411 and soon attracted learned men. By 1754 when the Royal and Ancient Golf Club of St. Andrews was founded, the city and royal burgh was world famed as a capital of learning and religion.

Because of golf's exposure in infancy to reading, writing and arithmetic, much of golf's lore has been authenticated although some primitive items have been played by hunch and by ear. The origin of the game itself is one of those developments lost in the remote mists of history when our species, emerging into its so-called human stage, hit things with sticks in playful, inconsequential performances instinctively exercised as training for self-preservation.

One legend has the Roman legionnaires bringing a game similar to golf into the wilds of Caledonia. It's possible. Caesar's special service officers also had the problem of tranquilizing troops that were bitching about, among other topics, "what was the big idea of those bubble-headed bastards in Rome sending us to this Jupiter-damned spot."

Paintings, stained-glass windows in cathedrals and casual phrases in books had golf, or something like it, originating in the Netherlands and France. Possibly, as relics of St. Andrew were brought to Scotland from Greece, the Greeks also had a name and a game for golf that came north with pioneer missionaries.

Naturally, due to proximity to Scotland and maybe because of the growing practice of keeping records (then, as now, due to the necessity of protecting the citizen against the tax commissars) the Dutch also have received credit for inventing golf. The Dutch *kolven* was played on ice, mainly, with a condensed version of it, similar to competition on a putting green, being played on small land areas.

The Dutch version of golf made its first American appearance prior to 1657. In that year, playful residents of Fort Orange (now Albany, N.Y.) seemingly got roaring drunk at *kolven* on Sunday, broke windows with *kolven* balls, and got arrested. What happened after the players at *kolven* were registered on police station blotter, history doesn't tell.

The father of Charles Evans, Jr. (the redoubtable Chick) achieved in his own shy field honor comparable with that of his illustrious son. Chick was the first amateur to win the United States Golf Association's National Open and its National Amateur Championship the same year, 1916. His father, who definitely never was known familiarly as Chick, Sr. was the noted librarian and bibliographer whose research and recording of American printed matter is basic material for historians.

Evans, Sr., discovered that in the 1790's there were several references to golf societies in South Carolina, Georgia, and Virginia. He surmised that due to the St. Andrews Society being devoted to the happy recollection of the customs of the fatherland and attaching them to the adopted home, it is probable that golf courses were fairly common in the area later known as the United States, shortly after 1733 when the St. Andrews Society in this country was founded.

For the golfer who wants to take a studious swing at golf history, the basic books are "A History of Golf", by Robert Browning, E.P. Dutton & Co., Inc., editor of the English magazine, Golfing, from 1910 to 1955; and "Fifty Years of American Golf", by H. B. Martin, Dodd, Mead & Co., a New York newspaper golf writer and cartoonist who wrote and illustrated several golf instruction books as the by-line author and as ghost. He was also Walter Hagen's first manager.

It is tradition for every professional golf champion to write an instruction book. It doesn't make any difference whether the playing star has credentials as an experienced teacher. Somebody gets the idea there's money in eagles teaching turtles to fly. So out comes another golf book bearing the name of a fine honest young person who does very little else but play golf hence, in some mysterious manner, is supposed to qualify as an authority on teaching golf.

In case you happen to be a sure enough bookworm

about golf you will pore over the pages of The Badminton Library's volume on golf, mainly written and
altogether edited by Horace Gordon Hutchinson (born
London, 16th May, 1859), a "stylish and attractive player," winner of the British Amateur championship in
1886 and 1887, and the first Englishman to captain the
Royal and Ancient.

That kindergarten book on golf is an astonishing volume, showing you many, many times that what you think
is new actually is old stuff. Badminton's "Golf" writers
often tell simple truths of technique that apparently are
eternal verities of golf despite changes in ball construction, shaft and clubhead modernization and altered conditions of play. Anyone who pretends to be a golf scholar
and hasn't read the Badminton volume on golf, published
by Longmans, Green and Co., in London in 1890, is
like the man who never had delirium tremens; he ain't
been no place and ain't seen nothin'.

Another of the exceptionally interesting golf books
was that of Fred Pignon, for years golfing correspondent
of the London Daily Mail, and manager of the 1931
British Ryder Cup team, in collaboration with Charles
G. Mortimer, a literary golf enthusiast. The result of
their research and writing is "The Story of the Open
Championship — 1860 to 1950." Their Open is the British Open, of course.

The growth of golf's publicity, as amateurs who played
for fun were shoved out of print by skilled, toiling mercenaries, is seen as the British Open became a competition for specialists who were halted in their march only
by triumphs of such rare geniuses as the amateurs John
Ball in 1890, Harold Hilton in 1892 and 1897 and the
greatest, Mr. R. T. Jones, U.S.A., in 1926, 1927 and
1930.

There is no book telling the story of the United States

Golf Association's National Open, although that top championship reflects the history of American golf from 1895 when the Open was played as a one-day (October 4) 36-hole affair on the nine-hole course of the Newport (R.I.) Golf Club. The initial U.S.G.A. Open was played with a field of ten professionals and one amateur during the same week the first National Amateur was played.

Notes in the Record Book of U.S.G.A. championships provide a big bank of basic material although much of the early data isn't recorded and probably has vanished forever.

The U.S.G.A. National Open of 1898, the first one played at 72 holes, is in the book as having 49 entries, only 29 of whom were listed with the scores. Whether there was a cut in the field after 36 holes, as later became the procedure, isn't told. The competition was played June 17 and 18 over the nine-hole course of the Myopia Club at Hamilton, Mass., which meant eight rounds of the course, before Fred Herd, professional at Washington Park Course in Chicago, won. This was the first U.S.G.A. National Open to be played separately from the National Amateur.

Yardage and par of the National Open courses were not given in the U.S.G.A. Record Book until 1941 when the first National Open in the south was played on the 7,005 yard, par 70 course of the Colonial Club at Fort Worth.

The Master's tournament that Bob Jones and Clifford Roberts created in 1934 on the magnificent Augusta (Ga.) National Golf Club course — also a glory that Jones and Roberts dreamed up — provides material for another history on the golf shelf. The scenery, the cast and the plots of Masters dramas are entertainingly told in word and picture. There is only slight reference to the business management of the Masters which has been a hobby of Roberts, master-mind of financing and directing giant corporations. Nobody but Roberts, Jones and a few of their companions in the Augusta National roster ever will know the business story of the Masters, the most successful of all golf tournaments and the tournament which pushed pros into realms of prestige and plutocracy far beyond the frontiers George S. May opened for them with his first big-money Tam o' Shanter tournaments in suburban Chicago.

It is regrettable that professional golf in the United States has practically no recorded history except the minimum of vague tournament data, flashing highlights of such personalities as Hagen, Hogan, Hutchison, Sara-

Hollanders appear to have played their game on ice

zen, Snead, Armour and a few more playing stars of lesser brilliance. Even the records of the Professional Golfers Association championships are inadequate and obviously incorrect. Officially the P.G.A. is indifferent to the fact that no other group of professional sportsmen has had the favorable effect on American social and economic life that professional golfers have registered.

Golf in the 90s in the United States was a pastime for Scotch immigrants and their curious neighbors and a fad for that olympus of American Society, Newport. It was getting nowhere as a pasture shinny; it perplexed passing teamsters and bruised otherwise contented cows. The game was in a questionable category with Scotch whisky which several Americans had tried and found a weak substitute for substantial belly-warming bourbon, the drink favored by the free in the land of the brave. The Scots were good, clean respectable people with their funny game but what could you expect of men who ate oatmeal and haggis and in their homeland wore skirts? Thus the native Americans viewed golf until the pioneer golf professionals brought the game out of that precarious condition, and by manners and means now vanishing into myth, established golf not only as a great aid in the pursuit of happiness but as a sport exercising tremendous influence on American social and economic life.

The golf club, as it centered around the old time pro and was nursed by him and flourished, popularized suburban living and before long had $100 per acre farms selling as costly country estates. With the rich and the socially ambitious living near a country club, suburban roads and suburban train service were improved. Sports bodies became "the thing" on automobiles. Sports fashions for men and women became part of the American

Organized links and clubhouses were unknown at first. Conveniently situated taverns served the purpose then

picture. Locker room men, doubling as country club bootleggers, overheard market tips and got wealthy, only to crash in 1929 with many of the biggest spending members.

The older professionals saw all this and were part of it. In many instances they were men primarily responsible for the development. Up to a few years ago, dozens of the professionals who built American golf were vigorous veterans with bundles of clippings, pictures, booklets and keen memories, fine equipment for a unique and merry story of an American sport.

The professionals' own organization, repeatedly importuned to collect and chronicle the history of their colleagues' substantial contribution to the United States, slumbered on.

An amusing sidebar to the failure of the P.G.A. to identify its members as *sui generis* in the professional sports scheme of things involved Ronald Teacher, a distinguished distiller of Scotch whisky. That worthy gent endowed the P.G.A. Seniors' Tournament after listening to Fred Corcoran, formerly P.G.A. tournament Bureau manager, tell of the old golf pros' long and happy influence on the socially and financially elevated class of Americans. The association of the Scotch distiller and the old golf pros has been in thoroughly excellent taste. That has not always been the case with tournament sponsors' use of golf for sales promotion. There are more rounds of drinks bought than of golf played at the more than 7,000 golf courses in the United States. Among the tournament professionals exists a far greater thirst for money than for alcoholic beverages, yet the P.G.A. warily backs away from additional tournament sponsorship by alcoholic beverage concocters.

BIG SPONSORSHIP AND BIG MONEY

Growth of tournament sponsorship is part of American golf history that abounds in untold stories. Hal Sharkey, a Newark, N. J., newspaperman who went on the pioneering winter junkets of the pros to California, Texas and Florida, was the first man to handle tournament booking and management. He did the chore as a sideline and turned the small percentage of prize money that he got for this work back to assessed contributors, many of whom needed eating, sleeping and moving money.

Robert E. Harlow, son of a New England minister, left a New York City newspaper sports department to manage the golf business affairs of Walter Hagen. The word "manage" is used loosely. Harlow and Hagen had more fun out of golf and golf business than any other two men ever have had in making a living at any sport. They put into golf much more than they took out and even with Harlow's missionary temperament and Hagen's refusal to think of money as the root of any worry, their collaboration brought them money easier than if they'd printed it. Harlow also was counselor and aide to that very canny juvenile Horton Smith, notwithstanding the fact that young Mr. Smith at all stages of his career could teach Hagen and Harlow things about handling money that they never imagined — or probably didn't care about, their idea was that the reason for money was to spend it.

After Harlow had established the P.G.A. Tournament Bureau, introduced such innovations as bringing a team of Japanese professionals to tour the United States and otherwise got the pros' toes in the doors of international business, a family fight in the P.G.A. threw him out.

Hagen, Harlow and Horton Smith are the three whose names should be revered by the world's tournament professionals today for their direction at a critical stage when the playing specialists could have been detoured from today's opulence.

Fred Corcoran succeded Harlow as the master impresario of tournament golf and put it into the multi-million dollar international business class. He has headed the P.G.A. Tournament Bureau, directed tournaments of the Ladies P.G.A., formed the International Golf Association for John Jay Hopkins, then head of General Dynamics, arranged the first tour of U. S. women professionals to Britain as an American dressmaker's advertising operation, originated the Teacher's Scotch international senior professional tournament, steered Sam Snead into fiscal championship among the tournament professionals and keeps himself engaged in busi-

When what is now Albany, New York, was under the control of the Dutch, people were fined for playing golf in the streets

ness concerns of several golf and baseball stars and in National Hockey League public relations.

THE ORIGIN OF THE CLUB AND THE COURSE

Record of the social history of golf begins in 1744 when "several Gentlemen of Honour, skillfull in the ancient and healthful exercise of Golf," petitioned the City of Edinburgh to provide a silver club for annual competition on the links of Leith. Twelve golfers entered the tournament but only ten showed for play. The winner of the first club competition was John Rattray, an Edinburgh surgeon. A golf club was a group of golfers that had duly elected officers, according to the founding fathers.

The Blackheath (England) club, formed in 1766 is

202

the first golf club outside of Scotland. The oldest existing American club is the Royal Montreal Golf Club which was founded in 1873. There is published record of a golf club holding meetings in 1786 at Charleston, S. C., but that club long ago diappeared.

Anyone who wants to exert a little effort at book dealers or in libraries can read interesting chronicles of the economic aspects of golf; the courses, the playing equipment and the development of the spectator-presentation of the game, as well as the growth of employment for playing specialists.

There doesn't seem to have been any trouble about getting land for golf courses. The good Lord took care of the fundamentals, of course, of golf architecture at St. Andrews on the bayshore pasture of the North Sea links where shepherds improvised golf while the gods were sheep-sitting and there wasn't much entertainment for the guardian Scots. Sheep and golfers always seem to have been able to get by contentedly on land good for nothing else but them.

Golf architecture had its origin in designs created when early golfers hacked turf off primitive seaside courses and prevailing winds did the rest in magnifying these scars into bunkers. Naturally the greens were the most prominent and intriguing targets in the landscape and that accounted for older, famous courses being planned (if you can call their architecture "planned") backwards. From greens to tees was the procedure in laying out most of the pioneer courses across the seas from Scotland.

Willie Park, Jr. renowned as the deadliest putter back in the time when greens were not the carpets they are today, was architect of more than 100 courses in the United States. He died back home in Edinburgh in 1925, reputedly of overwork in course construction and design work in the United States and Canada. Donald Ross, an immigrant from Dornoch, Scotland, was the first professional at Pinehurst, N. C. where Leonard Tuft, son of the founder, James W. Tuft, had staked out nine holes and tees in 1896. Ross came to the pine hills in 1900 and began improving and adding to the golf facilities and otherwise developing golf at Pinehurst so it became the American counterpart of St. Andrews. When Pinehurst visitors returned to their homes as golf evangelists they had Ross design their new courses.

Almost all of the pioneer professionals in the United States were golf course designers and builders. They also saw that the courses were mowed; they sold balls and clubs and bags, made and reshafted clubs, remolded the cut and battered gutta percha balls that were in use prior to 1900 and primarily instructed members and caddies in the technique, spirit and vernacular of the game.

Golf architecture was a part of the job the early American pro, generally, didn't welcome. He figured that if a course was much good the Almighty designed it. Considering the variation in terrain between the dunes of the Scotch littoral and the American meadows or farmland a golf course, as the Scots knew a golf course, was hard to simulate west of the Atlantic or anywhere else.

Willie Dunn, a young Scot who was building an 18-hole course at Biarritz, France, met W. K. Vanderbilt, Edward S. Mead and Duncan Cryder and was brought over by them to the United States in 1891 to build Shinnecock Hills Golf Club course on Long Island, near the Shinnecock Indian reservation.

Some elevations that Dunn thought were Indian burial mounds were left as bunkers. After wear and tear of those bunkers vigorous niblick shots began bringing up pieces of deceased whiskey bottles.

American amateur golfers were not content with the results of the casual, hasty course design of trail-blazing pros. Charles Blair Macdonald, a transplanted Scot who was one of the founders of the Chicago Golf Club and the first National Amateur champion of the United States, became the first golf architectural specialist when he designed the Chicago club's second course. Chicago Golf Club's first course was a 9-hole experiment which was outgrown after one summer. In 1893 the club bought farmland at Wheaton in west suburban Chicago and on that ground Macdonald set the first 18-hole course in the United States. It had two other distinctions. It was the first course in the world to have out-of-bounds. Previously, no matter on whose property the ball landed it was still on the golf course. The other point, unique at that time, was that the course played clockwise. Macdonald was a chronic slicer and made certain that it was going to be the hookers who hit the ball off the club's real estate.

Macdonald developed as a golf architect and designed several remarkably fine courses in the United States and Mid-Ocean in Bermuda. He inspired several other ardent and studious amateur golfers among them George W. Crump, the genius primarily responsible for Pine Valley in the Jersey sandhills not far from Philadelphia. Those who have been privileged to play Pine Valley pronounce it one of the world's greatest golf courses — or one of the world's worst. It definitely is not a dull course. Some citizens think Picasso is for fences and small vertical walls; others think Michelangelo is the king of corn. So what's art? And golf architecture should be, but not too often is, art.

Unfortunately the two informative books on the golf course architectural aspects of U. S. golf history are out of print. They are "Golf Course Architecture in

America" by George B. Thomas, Jr., and "The Links" by Robert Hunter, Jr.

Shot values have been altered by the longer ball, the improved shafts, the wedges, vastly improved greens and fairways, milder rough, uniform sand in bunkers, excellent drainage of most Class A courses, fairway watering, wider fairways and easier undulations of greens to fit motorized mowing. Nevertheless, the architectural principles that applied to interesting and tested course design then, still account for the difference between a good and a bad hole.

An appalling amount of money is wasted yearly in American golf by course alteration dictated by unqualified club officials by fee course operators. The private club alterations usually are revised in a few years by another committee which repeats the waste. That's a part of almost every club history.

THE HISTORY OF THE BALL
FROM WOOD TO RUBBER

One foggy area in golf history opens long enough to disclose the appointment, in 1618, by King James VI, of James Melville as a golf ball maker. From this and other circumstantial evidence historians surmise that at that time the most desirable golf balls were made of wood. The Dutch were skilled at wood-turning and then drew enough money out of Scotland to make the drain of the ball trade painful.

Whether or not the earlier golf balls were preferably wood, the most popular golf ball later on until nearly 1850 was a leather-covered ball stuffed with feathers. An expert could jam a tall hatful of feathers into the cover, then sew the cover together neatly and durably into a ball not much larger than the present size.

The next stage of golf ball development came after 1850 when the gutta percha ball was introduced. When

The first golf balls were stuffed with feathers

it was discovered that a scarred ball went farther than a smooth round one, then began the research in golf ball marking that continues to this day. Among the yarns about the gutta ball innovation was that the invention resulted from a St. Andrews golfer experimenting with a substance that had been wrapped around a small idol to protect it during shipment from a Scottish soldier in India to a relative in bonny Scotland.

The first of the modern type of golf ball was the rubber-cored ball wound by rubber thread. This type of construction was invented by Coburn Haskell of Cleveland, assisted by Bertram Work of the Goodrich Rubber Company at Akron and ingenious young men in the factory. The ball was marketable in 1898 but couldn't break the Scotch ballmakers' hold on the market until J. H. Taylor, on an American tour, hit the new ball at the Rockaway Hunt Club. The first shot he made was longer than any he'd hit before. He hit one onto a green 240 yards away and that made him a believer. But it was Sandy Herd who first won the British Open with the rubber-cored, thread-wound ball. He won in 1902 with 307 at Hoylake, two less than Braid's score at Muirfield the year before. In 1902 the Haskell ball was played by the winner of the U.S.G.A. National Open, Laurie Auchterlonie. His winning score was 78-78-74-77 — 307. That was the first time 80 was broken in all four rounds by the winner of the Open.

Harry Vardon said that scoring in the five years preceding the use of the rubber-cored ball in the British Open and in the first five years of the new ball's use showed that the ball meant at least three strokes per round improvement to any golfer.

THE CLUBS FROM TIMBER TO STEEL

The history of club improvement also is fuzzy. A very cautious approval of the steel shaft came from the U.S.G.A. when, in 1924, it OKed steel-shafted putters. The Western Golf Association was first to legalize the steel shaft, then the U.S.G.A. Not until November 1928 did the Royal and Ancient accept the steel shaft. Billy Burke was the first winner of a National Open to use a completely steel-shafted set of clubs. The clubs with which he beat George Von Elm in a 72-hole play-off at Inverness, Toledo, in 1931, were presented by Burke to the U.S.G.A. Museum.

An adjustment of golf to the conditions accounted for the introduction of the steel shaft. The inevitable development was stubbornly resisted by the U.S.G.A. and the Royal & Ancient. Hickory for shafts was getting scarce. Conditioning of the timber required a considerable investment in stock and time. Then, when the hickory was available as shaft stock the shortage of labor skilled in converting the raw sticks into finished golf shafts, the frequent breakage of shafts and the steadily increasing demand of more players playing more golf, all meant that the use of substitute materials was inevitable.

The Western Golf Association then was not much concerned about what the United States Golf Association or the Royal and Ancient Golf Club of St. Andrews thought about their sovereignty. The Western Association went along with the rules because compliance happened to be comfortable.

Horton Manufacturing Company, a New England maker of steel fishing rods, had been in the experimental manufacture of steel golf shafts for a couple of years and hired a former professional, Herbert Lagerblade, to conduct testing and marketing efforts. This writer's brother, Joe Graffis, then advertising manager of a golf magazine in Chicago, arranged with Western Golf Association officials to have the steel shaft tested to determine whether or not it had a place in golf.

Albert W. Gates was then president of the Western organization. He was a distinguished lawyer, a fine looking gentleman and a bon vivant.

The test was to take place at the Edgewater Golf Club in Chicago. Chick Evans, a member of that club, Alan Gow, its professional, and Bob Macdonald, then one of the nation's foremost golf stylists, were to do the testing. The spring day was chilly and chips of sleet bit with the wind. Mr. Gates and other Western officials, accompanied by a couple of quarts of genuine Scotch released from the pre-prohibition treasure of a gentleman sportsman, opened services in the clubhouse.

Evans, who never drinks, was eager to get the tests going. Eventually the professionals and reporters got

In France they had a game which consisted of knocking the ball along the roadways with a knobbed stick

out to the first tee where Evans, Gow and Lagerblade were hitting balls with the steel-shafted club.

At last, having protected themselves against the elements with the delicious and illegal anti-freeze, Mr. Gates and his fellow officers and Bob Macdonald came from the clubhouse to the first tee which was only a few yards away from a boundary fence to the right.

Macdonald was handed a steel-shafted driver. He blew on his cold hands. His hands then must have felt good. They were smelling of the best Scotch that had flavored the air of that tee in a couple of years.

Macdonald loosened up with a couple of practice swings.

Then he belted one with the steel-shafted tool. It sailed

far out then bent gently to the right and drifted over the fence.

"Outta bounds!" yelled a bundled caddy who'd been shagging the previous shots.

Mr. Gates gazed judiciously as the slice curved into the bordering street.

"Obviously the steel shaft does not alter the character of the game," said Mr. Justice Gates of the Western Golf Association's supreme court.

End of test. The steel shaft thereupon was official with the Western. Remaining formalities of the test were completed inside, along with that beautiful Scotch.

Several years later, with much more trouble and no better Scotch, the U.S.G.A., then the R. & A. followed the Western in making the steel shaft legal.

THE SAGA OF THE SIMPLE TEE

Another improvement in golf that brother Joe helped bring into golf while seeking an honest advertising dollar or two was the wooden peg tee, the original device invented by a New Jersey dentist named Lowell. The tee wasn't making any marketing headway against the cheap sand supplied from a convenient box for the caddie or player to finger into a small mound for supporting the ball.

Then Joe suggested that Walter Hagen and Joe Kirkwood, then wandering on exhibition schedules five or six days a week, be engaged as demonstrators. For very little money and not many gross of tees Kirkwood, the trick shot pioneer, and the glamorous, merry Hagen made the Reddy tee standard operating procedure in less than a year.

Dr. Lowell had a patent that seemed to be so simple and strong that no infringement was possible. His basic patent was the concave top of the tee which would hole the ball. When you think of the billions of tees with concave tops that have been used since the doctor's first-hand-whittled job, you may wonder how he could have missed making a fortune. Patent law suits took all his tee sales revenue, then some.

Not many years after Dr. Lowell invented his Reddy tee, a man went into the United States Patent Office records and found more than 100 patents on tees. Designs and materials ranged almost as far as the boundaries of imagination. One tee was made of a composition of fertilizer, grass seed and soil. The idea was that when the tee was broken and the turf beneath it scarred, repair work by nature would begin immediately.

GROOVING THE CLUBFACE

There have been several historic debates about the legality of clubs, with official bodies fearing that certain variations from the old stuff might be dangerous departures from "the traditional and customary form and make." The first of these governmental worries was about the center-shafted "Schenectady" putter that Walter Travis used when he won the British Amateur championship in 1904. The R. & A. barred it as a device of the devil, whereupon there was a gigantic (for those days) increase in the sale of center-shafted putters, and putting continued to be no better than before. Eventually the Royal and Ancient abandoned its stand against the type of putter that the short-hitting Americanized Australian had used in defeating the long-hitting Edward Blackwell.

Another question of the legality of clubs popped up in 1921 when Jock Hutchison, a professional transplanted from St. Andrews to the United States, defeated British amateur Roger Wethered for the British Open title, after a play-off. The facts were that the Hutchison victory

212

came at what actually was his home course and then only because Wethered stepped on his ball while backing up to take his stance. On the hard greens at St. Andrews, Hutchison had stopped his approach shots with back-spin that the R. & A. thought must have been the result of grooves that bit into the golf ball so trickily that a talented operator like Hutchison could have the ball spinning back almost like a yo-yo.

So the R. & A. went into labor and brought forth a ruling against sharply grooved irons. The U. S. G. A. also went to great scientific pain to make studies and measurements and rulings so precise that authorities sat around at National Open championships making micrometric investigations of grooving in clubs. This caused considerable confusion to players who had done hopeful filing of club-faces expecting some magic which neither they nor the U. S. G. A. could clearly explain.

The comical and embarassing part of the club face-scoring affair popped out of investigations made by the U. S. G. A. Implements and Ball Committee several years ago. The tests showed that just as much backspin could be put on a ball by a mirror-smooth iron clubface manipulated by an expert as could be produced by the sharply ribbed faces with which Hutchison wrought evil in the 1921 British Open.

Still another amusing sector of golf club designing history is that involving the wedge. Scotch prototypes of the tool are in the U. S. G. A. and other golf museums and in private collections of old clubs. Scotch course conditions and the Scotch type of play which accented manipulation of the club didn't provide much of a demand for the flange-soled club utimately known in the United States, then around the golfing world, as the wedge.

A foresighted Texan devised a wedge that he believed would get the leading edge of the club under the ball so the "sweet spot" of clubhead weight would propel the ball up and along the desired trajectory. The inventor got Horton Smith interested in the idea. The Burke Golf Company made a line of iron clubs using the design principle. While the clubs were satisfactory they weren't sensationally successful in shot execution and as they looked too far away from the current type of iron club head they vanished from the market only to reappear some years later as the basis of conventional wedge design.

Smith used the flanged niblick with decidedly more effectiveness than the customary type of niblick could be used. Gene Sarazen saw the club and got the brilliant, sound hunch of putting more metal on the flange and rounding the flange so it would come under the ball, through the sand and up out of it, shoveling the ball out with the sand. Smith was doing very well with the original sand wedge, Sarazen did better with his accented version and Johnny Revolta came along and used the implement like a magic wand.

With the development of the wedge the terrors of sand traps vanished.

THE EVOLUTION OF THE RULES

Development of the rules of golf reveals that golfers must have been wiser than they realized. The game, with its playing grounds of infinite variety, presents complex problems of legislation which add up to giving the golf ball instead of the golfer the benefit of any ruling.

Other games played on uniform fields have more rules than golf has. The golfer who has not read the rules of the game and who says they are too many and too perplexing must be embarrassed to learn the rules of golf

214

Charles I was said to have played golf at Newcastle while he was confined there

are fewer than those of baseball and football.

Nobody has been able to locate the first rules of golf. Many golfers don't seem to have been able to locate any rules. They play as happens to make what they call their score look better. Their procedure provoked a newly immigrated professional to remark about members at the midwestern club where he had been hired, "This is different from the game they play in Scotland. There they hit the ball around the course; here you carry it around."

Tommy Armour made a sharp comment on rules at the first tee at Boca Raton after a filibuster preceding the arranging of wagers.

"Now that we've agreed on larceny according to our respective hopes, what sort of a game are we going to play; golf or whatever that thing is that you fellows make up as you go along?" asked the sardonic Silver Scot.

The first rules of which written record has been discovered are those codified at Leith a decade prior to May 14, 1754 when 22 "Noblemen and Gentlemen of St. Andrews" met to establish rules for their trophy play and took "Articles and Laws in Playing the Golf" from regulations used by the Silver Club of the City of Edinburgh and before that at Leith. There were 13 of these rules. To this day they are basically the rules of the game with the exception of the old first rule which called for teeing the ball within a club-length of the hole and a later one removing the early penalty for getting into casual water.

Regulations governing ball and club specifications are comparatively recent. The British ball has the same

Scotsmen originated the idea of cross-country play

weight limitations as the U. S. G. A. ball "not greater than 1.62 ounces avoirdupois" but must have size "not less than 1.620 inches in diameter" while the U. S. G. A. legalizes a larger ball of "size not less than 1.680 inches in diameter."

In recent years there was discussion in Britain about increasing the ball to the American size, but after considerable talk, between the Royal and Ancient officials, British P. G. A. officers and playing experts and ball manufacturers, the subject was dropped. The authorities came to the conclusion there actually wasn't any appreciable difference in the playing qualities of the two types of balls even though the lighter British ball might conceivably lie a bit better on the close British turf.

The United States had one costly experiment with a larger and lighter "balloon" ball in 1931. Nobody liked it and after its short life it was abandoned, unmourned. Its lesson to quit diddling around with ball specifications and to keep in mind that the main point is what the players do to the ball rather than what the ball does to the players also is disappearing, so some golfers suspect. However, getting exceedingly technical about the game is a lot of fun of a worried sort. The U. S. G. A. feels compelled to view with alarm the minority who can and dare to hit the ball hard since the rough has been minimized as a hazard biting those boys who do hit long and wild. There have been no cases of protest against undue length of the golf ball registered by any of the 99 per cent of golfers who never will be able to hit the ball hard enough to hurt it, or themselves.

Limitation of clubs to 14 was ordered by the U. S. G. A. to become effective January 1, 1938. The Royal and Ancient announced a similar limitation effective on the same date.

There have been protests from playing professionals

against that restriction. They want the allowable number raised to 16. Which 16 nobody knows. The majority of professionals have two woods, a driver and a brassie, in the bag. The amateurs, according to the makers of head covers, have a 1-, 3-, 4-, and 5- wood. The professionals now go for wedges almost as much as the earlier tournament professionals liked woods. Toney Penna, when a youthful clubmaker, made four drivers for Leo Diegel; one with a hook, another with a slice, one to drive with the wind, and another against it.

Harry Cooper carried 26 clubs. Lawson Little carried 30. Rarely did—or does—any professional expert with all his finesse use more than eight clubs and a putter per round. But what eight clubs?

Perhaps this controversy is one that will die a peaceful death unless bothersome and bird-brained parties keep the debate stirred. There were gaps between the playing professionals and the amateurs concerning the rules prior to 1965. Until it occurred to the professionals' advocates that unless professionals and amateurs played the same game sponsorship money from which, to pros all blessings flow, might be imperiled. Thereupon the smart mercenaries said "let's all be one happy family."

COMPETITION FOR
GOLFDOM'S SENIOR CITIZENS

Growth of senior golf organizations is a conspicuous sector of the game's history in the United States. Today almost all the national and sectional senior golf associations have waiting lists. The North and South Senior tournament which replaced the North and South Open at Pinehurst when the prize money demands became higher than the advertising value warranted, has a waiting list requiring applicants for entries to stand by for six or seven years. The Southern Seniors, Western Seniors and state groups of golfers, 55 or older, have about all the play they can handle in their tournaments.

The U. S. G. A. Senior Open Amateur championship has become one of the most attractive competitions in the country. Without polling seniors, the U. S. G. A. reduced its Seniors' championship age from 55 to 50. There was fiery protest. The U. S. G. A. wisely said, "our error; so sorry," and restored the original age limit. One result of that contretemps was to inspire the veteran Chick Evans to form the Golden Seniors' association. Scoring in the mid-seventies is necessary to make much of a showing in the first flight of this conclave of the elders.

Scoring one's age or better no longer is a noteworthy feat by professional or amateur golfers. Fred McLeod, 1908 National Open champion, has bettered his age from one to many times annually from his 68th birthday. William Diddle, several times Indiana State amateur champion, long ago, in his 81st year beat his age 31 times.

Financially the seniors score impressively. The most desirable golfing resorts have senior tournaments as features of their programs. Competition in these senior affairs is keen, and extends internationally.

American groups of seniors hold competitions with older golfers in Canada, Scotland, England, France and other European countries, in South Africa, Mexico and Japan. The wives of the nation's senior golfers now, usually, are golfers themselves. Establishing the U. S. G. A. Senior Women's Amateur championship in 1962 recognized the tremendous boom in women's golf which now accounts for more than a quarter of all the rounds played in a year in the United States.

Organization of senior golf began at the Apawamis Club, Rye, N. Y., in the winter of 1904, according to Horace L. Hotchkiss, founder of the United States

Seniors' Golf Association. That association was merrily informal as guests of Apawamis until 1917 when, at a dinner at Delmonico's, the gathering was made formal. So what had begun as a happy thought over the glowing bowl at Apawamis, became the senior golf movement of the world.

There are two rather comprehensive statistical and historical round-ups of the story of golf. One is "The Encyclopedia of Golf" compiled by Nevin H. Gibson. It mainly deals with championships and personalities in the United States.

The other collection of a wide range of golf information is The Golfer's Handbook. This is an annual of nearly 1100 pages which has been issued in Scotland for more than 60 years. This fat, red book has an immense supply of records, mainly of British major and minor events although the national and international championships of the United States and other nations are listed. It includes "Who's Who in Golf," the R. & A. Rules of Golf, directories of golf clubs in many countries other than the United States and miscellaneous material that answers a multitude of questions.

Included in The Golfer's Handbook stock of data are such items as the world record for holes-in-one (29 by Charles T. Chevalier, professional at Heaton Moor, England); the first lady golfer (Mary Queen of Scots, who was beheaded on 18 February, 1584); Balls in Strange Places, Bookmakers and Golf, Length of Championship Courses, Record Drives and How 18 Holes Became a Round.

The Handbook's background on the 18-hole round:

"Bruntsfield Links in the heart of the City of Edinburgh, the oldest course in the world where golf is still played, used to have only six holes, North Berwick seven, Gullane 13 and later 15, Musselbrugh five and

A hundred years ago golf courses had no official number of holes

later eight, the usual match being over two rounds or 16 holes, and Montrose 25. At Wimbledon, 1864 to 1870, the full course was seven holes; when Tom Dunn went to the course he enlarged it to 19 holes. Blackheath had seven holes and the usual match was three rounds to make 21 holes. Royal Aberdeen as late as 1875 only had 15 holes.

"When the first Open championship was played at Prestwick in 1860 the course consisted of 12 holes and three rounds were played to complete the 36 holes which was the championship test until 1891.

"At St. Andrews the game for generations was played nine holes out and the same nine greens were used for playing home. The accidental incident that 18 was the most convenient number of holes at St. Andrews, with

the gradually established pre-eminence of the place in golf, operated in the direction of 18 holes being accepted as the standard number for a round of golf."

So there goes into the grave of fact the beautiful legend that 18 holes became the standard round of golf because that was the length measured by the amount of whisky a true golfer carried as fuel.

This has been a Sunday recurrence from the time that golf was invented

INGENIOUS
GAMES WITHIN
THE GAME:
THEY'RE ALL GOLF

Competitions for variegating the entertainment in golf are many and ingenious. Some of them are fundamentally scoring procedures such as the Nassau system which gives a point for each nine and for the match. This method of scoring originated at the Nassau Country Club on Long Island. Other geographical labels are the Peoria system of handicapping and the Pinehurst selective drive partnership play. The Pinehurst idea was pushed up by Dick Chapman, former U.S. and British amateur champion. Dick's father and mother probably pioneered it in the United States but it was Dick and his wife, Eloise, who popularized the plan of selecting the preferable drive of two partners, then playing alternate shots into the cup. The procedure is extensively used in professional-amateur team play as well as in the co-educational events.

The Peoria handicapping system origin is vague. No golfer in Peoria knows who gave birth to the notion. It is simple and works well in events where players have no playing records on which handicaps are based. After the players tee off, six holes are selected for handicap computation purposes. A player's scores on these six holes are selected, multiplied by three and par is subtracted to determine the handicap.

The Callaway system also flowered in Pinehurst where the handicapping method's inventor, Lionel Callaway, has been a professional for many autumns, winters and springs. The Callaway and Peoria systems of one round handicapping are useful and generally very fair when one day tournaments are played by golfers who have no formal handicaps. Still another system of this sort is the Palm Beach Old Guard handicapping method devised by that golfing society's veteran secretary, William Langford. Variations of these systems under other names are devised and employed in efforts to thwart the evil designs of pot-hunters and hustlers who perform in their mysterious ways to demonstrate that golf is not always a gentleman's game.

Some years ago this writer began collecting ideas of competitive events to compile into a booklet for heads of men's and women's golf committees at clubs and for professionals. This was published by the National Golf Foundation and later was revised and enlarged by Rex McMorris, while operating head of the game's promotion bureau, and other members of the Foundation staff.

The Foundation's booklet, "Golf Events", is the source of practically all presentations of variety programs for play at golf clubs and the facts that follow are excerpted from it.

THE CALLAWAY SYSTEM OF ONE-ROUND HANDICAPPING One of the problems facing tournament committees organizing convention, resort or industrial golf tournaments, is that of selecting a fair method of one-round handicapping in those instances where participants have no established handicaps on which to determine net scores for prizes. The Callaway System of Automatic Handicapping is a recent development which offers an interesting solution to this problem, a solution that is becoming increasingly popular.

Under this method a player's handicap is determined after each round by his gross score for the 18 holes and by his worst, or highest, scores on individual holes.

For instance, if a player's gross score is 107, he turns to the table below and opposite that score finds that he may deduct the total of his four worst, or highest, individual hole scores. Thus, if he had scored one 9, two 7's and several 6's, he could deduct a total of 29 strokes, giving himself a net score of 78.

CLASS A

Gross Score	Deduct
Par or less	Scratch
One over par to 75	½ worst hole
76 to 80	Worst hole
81 to 85	Worst hole plus ½ next
86 to 90	Two worst holes
91 to 95	Two worst holes plus ½ next
96 to 100	Three worst holes

CLASS B

101 to 105	Three worst holes plus ½ next
106 to 110	Four worst holes
111 to 115	Four worst holes plus ½ next
116 to 120	Five worst holes
121 to 125	Five worst holes plus ½ next

CLASS C

126 to 130	Six worst holes
131 to 135	Six worst holes plus ½ next
136 to 140	Seven worst holes
141 to 145	Seven worst holes plus ½ next
146 to 150	Eight worst holes

Note: Worst hole equals highest hole score regardless of rated par of hole. Also, half strokes are counted to the nearest whole stroke...

ONE DAY EVENTS

AGE CONTEST

TWENTIES	AGES 20-29
THIRTIES	AGES 30-39
FORTIES	AGES 40-49
FIFTIES	AGES 50-59
SIXTIES	AGES 60 and over

All enter under the same conditions, play on the same day, on the same course and use their full handicaps. Each may choose his own partner, the partner, however, to be in the same class as himself. 18 Hole Medal Play, prizes to be awarded in each class.

ALIBI EVENT Contestant may replay the same number of shots as allowed by his handicap — but not more than one on any single hole and with the exception of putts.

AVERAGE SCORE Medal play. Partners average their gross scores for each hole and deduct half their combined handicap from their 18 hole total. Half strokes count as whole strokes after totaling.

BEST BALL AND AGGREGATE (LOW-BALL, LOW-TOTAL) This is a variation of the regular four-ball match. Two points are involved on each hole, one point for the best ball and one point for the low aggregate score of a side.

BEST BALL MATCH Each player plays his own ball. Two of the contestants are partners and play their best ball against the score of a third and generally better player.

BINGLE-BANGLE-BUNGLE Three points on each hole. One point to player whose ball first comes to rest on clipped surface of green. A second point to the player whose ball is nearest the cup after all players are on the green. The third point goes to the player who first sinks his putt. On short holes, where it is possible to reach the green from the tee, no point is awarded for first on the green, since the player with the honor has too great an edge; instead, this point goes to the player whose ball is second nearest to the pin after all balls are on the green. In settling up, each player wins the difference between his total points and the total points of each player with fewer points.

BLIND BOGEY Before leaving first tee each player estimates the handicap he needs to net a score between 70 or 80.

After all players have teed off, committee picks a 'blind' figure between 70 and 80 which remains secret until last player has turned in score card. The player whose net score is closest to the blind bogey is the winner.

BLIND HOLE MATCH Played under full handicap. Only scores to count are those shot on certain unannounced holes, generally 9 of the 18, mixed. Selection of holes not made by committee until field has left first tee.

BLIND LOW-NET FOURSOME Contestants play 18 holes with whom they please. At conclusion of play, committee draws names from hat and groups players into foursomes; net scores are added to determine winning foursome.

BLIND PARTNER EVENT May be almost any event, or may be staged as a non-interfering added feature of the day. After players have left the first tee, the committee makes pairings by lot. A golfer does not know with whom he will be paired until the round is over.

BREAKFAST TEAM TOURNEY All interested golfers assemble at the club for breakfast, then are split by handicaps into two equal teams. Low handicap golfer of Team A plays against low man of Team B, and so on until all contestants are paired. Play is in foursomes, medal play, no handicaps. Use Nassau scoring (see Nassau) to determine victors in each foursome, who get their breakfasts bought by losers.

CADDIE TOURNEY Open to all boys who are regular caddies. Generally scheduled on a Monday late in the season, but before school vacation ends. Boys play 18 holes in the morning for a variety of prizes and are given a picnic, athletic contests and souvenirs to round out the day. At some clubs, where caddies come from poorer neighborhoods, members donate clothing and shoes their sons have outgrown. Other members make a cash donation toward a large array of prizes boys like.

CHOICE SCORE The best score of the partners on each hole is used in arriving at their 18 hole total. Full or ¾ handicaps allowed and players enter their net scores in computing their round total.

BLIND CHOICE SCORE Same as above, except only half of the holes of the course (and the players do not know which ones) are used in determining the winners.

CLASS AND CLUB CHAMPIONSHIPS Class and club championships may be played on either a match play or medal play basis. No handicaps are figured.

If the championship is to be played on a match play basis usually a qualifying round of 18 or 36 holes is played with either the low 8 or the low 16 players qualifying for match play. If the championships are be to decided on a medal play basis this can be done either by playing 72 holes or 36 holes. Some clubs decide their championships on one day with the contestants playing 36 holes, others decide theirs on 72 holes, over four weekends of play.

Some clubs match their players according to handicaps without a qualifying round.

CLASS SYNDICATE TOURNAMENT This tournament is played in four classes: Class "A", Class "B", Class "C", and Class "D".

Each entrant has a chance to "get lucky" and win some syndicates. They are cumulative in each class. An entry fee is charged and turned over to the pro who furnishes credits on golf merchandise from the pro shop to the winners. The man who scores the lowest in each class on a hole wins the syndicate in his class for that particular hole. When there are ties on a hole, the syndicate for that hole goes to the man winning the following hole. If there are two or more holes in a row tied, the syndicates for all of the tied holes go the man having the next win. In other words, the syndicates on tied holes are cumulative and go to the man making the first win following the tied hole.

The entry fee for each class is divided into 18 parts, one for each hole. For example, if the entry fee is 50¢ and there are 20 entries in one class, the total entry fee would be $10.00. This $10.00 is divided by 18, making the amount of syndicate per hole 55¢. Therefore, if a man wins 6 syndicates he will win a total of $3.30 which he receives in golf merchandise, as explained above. This makes a fine yearly spring event, before handicaps have been fixed, as it provides a tournament with prizes without the use of handicaps.

CLUB CHAMPIONSHIP POOL The following was found to add interest to the usual Men's Club Championship:

One thousand tickets, with detachable stubs are printed and numbered from 1 to 1000. These are sold prior to the tournament.

All entrants are then seeded and numbered from one up. The one thousand stubs are placed in a jar, from which someone draws one at a time, the same number of stubs as there are entrants. The first stub drawn gets No. 1 seeded player, the second one No. 2, etc.

The tournament is then played and the pool money divided as follows:

To the holder of the winner's stub, 40 per cent in merchandise from golf shop.

To the holder of the runner-up's stub, 30 per cent in merchandise from golf shop.

To the holders of the two semi-finalists' stubs, 15 per cent each in merchandise from golf shop.

COSTUME TOURNAMENT Mixed Scotch Foursomes. Each player dresses in some sort of costume of his own selection. Prizes can be awarded for best costumes as well as best scores.

GET-ACQUAINTED TOURNEY 18 hole medal play with handicaps. Each entrant must play with a partner with whom he has never before been teamed.

HIGH AND LOW BALL Two points are involved on each hole. One point is scored for the best ball and one for the best of the two poorest balls, in regular four-ball match. For example, A and B are partners and C and D are partners. A scores 5 and B scores 3 on a hole. C and D each score 4 on the same hole. A and B win a point for the best ball and C and D win a point because their second best ball is better than A.

HUSBAND & WIFE TWO-BALL MATCH This is to be played the same as a Two-Ball Mixed Foursome, but the partners must be husband and wife.

JUNIOR TOURNEY Open to sons and wards of members below the age of 18. Medal play, 18 or 36 holes, no handicap. In addition to an award for low score among the entire field, it is a good idea to have several flights by age groupings. Where enough daughters are regular club players, a junior tourney for them is suggested.

KICKERS' REPLAY TOURNAMENT Each player is allowed to replay any and only two shots in a round. The player must continue with the replayed ball once it is called. Full handicap to apply.

LONG AND SHORT TOURNEY Many players have good long games and poor short games, and vice-versa. This event combines the ability of these two types of golfers. One player does the driving and long work, his partner does the approaching and putting. Players select their own partners.

LOW-NET FOURSOME The total score of the four players, less handicaps, determines the winning foursome in the field of contestants.

MILLION DOLLAR TOURNAMENT For this event the Club has printed sufficient script in units of $100 and $500 each (the majority in the $100 denomination) to furnish each entrant with $10,000 in script at the first tee on the day of the tournament. Usually one can get a local printer to make up this script with his small advertisment on the back.

Each entrant pays 25¢ or any amount you may designate, for use of the script, with a chance at the grand prize that goes to the player finishing with the most money.

The members may make up their own foursomes or ask the pro to arrange them. Each foursome will divide itself into teams and use the following system of scoring:

    2 points for low ball
    1 point for low total
    3 points for a birdie
    5 points for an eagle

(If eagle or birdie is scored, low ball does not count.)

Each foursome will elect a captain who is to decide all bets and arguments and to keep time on lost balls. Captain will turn in money after the 18th hole, recording the total of high man in the foursome.

Players incurring one of the following penalties must pay the sum named to each of the other players in his foursome:

    $100 for playing into rough
    $200 for playing into wrong fairway or hitting tree and bouncing into right fairway
    $300 for missing ball entirely
    $300 for swearing
    $100 for stopping to look for tee
    $300 for loss of ball — to be paid to each member who helps look for it — hunting time, two minutes limit.
    $300 from each member of foursome to player whose ball is: first on the green; first down.

Players are to be admonished not to borrow nor to give away money to a big winner, but to play fair. Only cash counts for the prize, which can be an article of merchandise or credit for merchandise from the pro shop.

This is another very fine tournament to either start or wind up the season.

MINIATURE TOURNEY A 36 hole event. Contestants, using ¾ of their handicaps, play nine holes in morning to qualify. Entire field then divided into flights of eight players each, the eight low net players forming the first flight, the next eight low net players forming the second flight, etc. Three match play rounds of nine holes each are then played to determine a winner and runner-up for each flight.

MIXED FOURSOMES Good for Sunday afternoons. Partners consist of one man and one woman. Man drives from odd numbered tees, the woman from even numbered tees (or vice versa). From tee to green, partners play every other shot. Allow half combined handicaps.

SELECTIVE DRIVE Same as above, except both man and woman drive from each tee. Either ball is continued in play; the other ball is picked up.

MIXED FOURSOME, POINT COMPETITION Selective drive, alternate shots: one-half combined handicaps to be used just as they come on the card.

MOST 3's Or 4's or 5's. Use net or gross scores, as you prefer. Can also be used in combination with other events.

MYSTERY EVENT Send players out without telling them what type of contest they are entering, except that it is either match or medal play. After all scores are in, release news of what the event was, and determine winner.

NASSAU (OR BEST-NINES) TOURNAMENT This is similar to the handicap medal play except that prizes are awarded for the best first nine, the best second nine, and the best 18 holes. Full handicap is used for 18 hole scores and half handicap for 9 hole scores. The advantage is that a player making a poor start, or tiring at the finish, may still win a prize for his play on the other nine.

NEVER-WAS-ER OR CONSOLATION TOURNAMENT Usually held at end of season and may be any type of event committee selects. Only players eligible to compete are those members who have not won a tournament prize during the season. Some clubs give a prize to every player in the tournament.

NO ALIBI TOURNAMENT Instead of deducting his handicap at the end of the round, each player is allowed to replay during the round the number of shots equaling three-quarters of his handicap. A stroke replayed must be used even if it is worse than the original; it cannot be replayed a second time.

ODD AND EVEN TOURNAMENT This tournament is played in foursomes; two players making up one team. One player to play all even holes and the other all odd holes. Use one-half of combined handicap; no more than 10 strokes difference in handicap of partners. Low net is the winner.

ONE-BALL EVENTS Very interesting events are those where only one ball is used by the partners, the two players stroking alternately between tee and green, and driving alternately from successive tees. Such one-ball events can be just about anything listed under individual play, but most effective novelty is secured by requiring special pairings. Among the combinations are: father and son, pro and amateur, mother and daughter, brothers, brother and sister, man and wife, member and guest, member and caddie. This last event is particularly recommended to clubs interested in fostering caddie good-will. A spirit of friendliness and understanding cannot be more easily secured.

PAR BATTLE Played under full handicap. Advise players that on a certain ten holes of the course five points will be won if par or better is shot. On three other holes award 10 points for par or better. On three other holes there is a 5 point penalty for players who do not score par or better, and on the remaining two holes, the penalty is 10 points for failing to make par. Winner is player with most points at end of round.

PARENT AND CHILD TOURNAMENT Parent may play with one or more children. Selected drive, alternate strokes; one-half combined handicap is used for 18 holes. A nominal entrance fee may be charged each team which may be used toward purchase of prizes.

This tournament is best held on Sunday, after regular play, not to start later than four o'clock. It can be followed by a buffet lunch, at which prizes can be presented.

PARI-MUTUELS Play in these events is in foursomes with full handicaps. Score for each hole is determined by the two best balls on each hole (net). The score of the best two balls is used rather than the score for the best ball, as the two-ball procedure keeps more players in the competition, playing out each hole.

Usually a dollar entry fee is charged for this event and this is used to buy the merchandise prizes for the winning foursome. When it is legal, bets on the foursomes to win, place or show are taken in units of one dollar. After the last foursome has left the first tee, the betting is closed and the total money, less 10%, the pro's cut for running the event, is divided into forty parts. The money is then split as follows:

	Win	Place	Show
WINNING FOURSOME	16 parts	8 parts	4 parts
SECOND PLACE FOURSOME		6 parts	3 parts
THIRD PLACE FOURSOME			3 parts

All of the bettors who have bet on the winning foursome to win divide the win-money. For instance, if the win-money was $100.00 and 8 men had bet $1.00 on them to win and one man had bet $2.00 on them to win, the $1.00 bettors would receive $10.00 each and the $2.00 bettor would receive $20.00.

POINT ACCUMULATION TOURNAMENT
To be scored as follows:
Any score equaling par or better, 5 points.
Any score from 1 to 4 strokes inclusive over par, 3 points.
Any score from 5 to 7 strokes inclusive over par, 1 point.
The 18th fairway is measured off at 150 yards, 175 yards, 200 yards and 250 yards.

A player with a handicap of 12 or less scores:
5 points for driving over 250 yards
4 points for driving over 200 yards
3 points for driving over 175 yards
1 point for driving in fairway
A player with a handicap of 13 or more scores:
5 points for driving over 200 yards
4 points for driving over 175 yards
3 points for driving over 150 yards
1 point for driving in fairway.
(All drives in order to score points must be in the fairway.)

Player scoring largest number of points is naturally the winner, but second and third prizes may also be given.

POINT TOURNEY Players are awarded 3 points for each birdie scored, 2 points for each par and 1 point for each hole played in one stroke over par. Played under full handicap; winner is golfer with most points at end of round.

PRO VS. MEMBERS The club professional agrees to play a handicap match against each member as he is challenged, making a nominal charge for each round. The professional plays from scratch. The member making the best showing in his match receives a prize from the professional at the end of the season.

PUTTING TOURNAMENT The two men making fewest putts in 18 holes each win a bag of shag balls. Entrance fee, 3 old balls.

RELAY TOURNAMENT In this tournament a player's score for the first nine holes is added to his partner's score for the second nine holes, with an allowance of ⅜ of their combined handicaps, to arrive at a net score for 18 holes.

RELAY EVENT Partners select one of their scores for the first nine, the other score for the second nine to get their 18 hole total. Allow ½ or ⅜ combined handicap.

REMORSEFUL GOLF In this contest each player has the privilege of making his opponent play over any four shots, during the round. These may be shots which he considers lucky or feels cannot be duplicated. For example, a player may hole out a 20 foot sidehill putt, at which point his opponent can say, "I respectfully request you to replay that shot" and he must replay it.

REPLAYED SHOT TOURNAMENT During this tournament each player has the option of replaying one shot on every hole. However, he must carry on from the replayed shot even though it be worse than the first one.

SCOREFEST Two teams, of any size. Losing team is the one that scores the least points on following system:

232

Net scores over 100	2 points
Net scores 90 to 100	5 points
Net scores 85 to 89	10 points
Net scores 80 to 84	15 points
Net scores 75 to 79	25 points
Net scores 70 to 74	40 points
Net scores under 70	75 points

SCOTCH FOURSOME Two players to a side. On each hole, there is a point for low ball and a point for low aggregate score of a side. Holes may be halved by all players making the same score, or by one side winning low ball and losing the aggregate. On some holes, only one point may be won, as for example if a side wins low ball and ties the aggregate. This event is sometimes played with low-ball worth two points and aggregate, one.

SCRATCH AND SCRAMBLE Four-ball Medal Play.

Example: A and B are partners. A's handicap is 10, B's handicap is 15, total combined handicap 25; divide by two and you have a handicap for each of 12½.

On each hole the scores of the two players are added and then divided by two, the result being the score of each for the hole. For instance A scores 5 and B scores 4, making a total of 9. This is divided by two, making the score of each for the hole 4½.

It will be most interesting if the Committee will draw the teams without regard for personal preferences of the members, combining a high handicap man with a low handicap man. This will bring together players who have never played together before. It will also give the poor players an opportunity to play with the better players and to learn more about the game and its rules.

SCRIPT TOURNEY Furnish each player with $10,000 in stage money. Each player has a partner; play in foursomes. Pair with the most script after play is over wins. Wins and losses settled whenever incurred during round. Awards are such matters as: low ball each hole, $100; low aggregate each hole, $200; birdies, $300; eagles, $500; first ball on each green, $100; first putt sunk, $200; etc., as the ingenuity of the committee can devise. Penalties include: ball in rough, $100; ball in wrong fairway, $300; ball hitting tree and rebounding into fairway being played, $500; ball in water, $200; fanning, $300; swearing, $400; swearing at caddie, $1,000, etc.

SELECTED SCORE Each contestant plays 36 holes during the day. From his 2 cards he can select his best score on each hole and apply his handicap. The player with the lowest net score for his 18 holes is, of course, the winner.

SENIOR TOURNEY Medal play, 18 holes. Open to players 50 or more years of age. Played without regular club handicaps, but older players get a stroke advantage as follows; 50 to 54 years old, scratch; 55 to 59, two strokes; 60 to 64, four strokes; 65 to 69, six strokes; 70 and over, eight strokes. There should be a prize for low gross player, no matter what his age.

SIX OR TWELVE HOLE ELECTIVE 9 or 18 holes medal play, at the end of which each player selects as his score the total scores made on his 6 or 12 best holes.

Two thirds of the regular club handicap is used for 18 holes; ⅓ for 9 holes.

SIX POINT MATCH Six points are at stake on each hole. In reality there are two points being fought for by each pair in the threesome — A vs. B, B vs. C, and A vs. C. Low score each hole wins 4 points, middle score wins 2 points, high man wins nothing. If all tie, 2 points apiece. Two players tie for low, 3 points each. One player, low, other two tied, the split is 4-1-1. Generally the point allocation is obvious, but when a player gets a stroke from one of his opponents and not from the other one, it is harder to figure the number of points each player wins. In such cases, merely compute results of each match (AB, BC, and AC) separately and the point split is readily determined.

SPECK TOURNAMENT Entry fee one golf ball. Every entrant has a chance to win two golf balls. Entries are divided into two-man teams.

Scoring as follows:

Longest ball on fairway	1 speck
First one on the green	1 speck
Closest ball to pin on approach shot	1 speck
One putt greens	1 speck
Lowest score on the hole	1 speck

Ties are split or canceled.

Count the total number of specks scored by each team and the team having the most number of specks wins the match from the team with which it is paired, each member of the winning team receiving 2 golf balls.

SPLASH CONTEST No entry fee, but players must contribute one new ball for every time they play into a water hazard during the round. A player entering contest but failing to turn in his score is charged 3 balls, on suspicion. Award balls to the three low net players on a 60-30-10 split-up.

SWEEPSTAKES Stroke (or medal) play, full handicap. Each player in tourney signs up for one new golf ball. Golfer with low net score wins half the balls, second best net takes one-third, third place wins one-sixth.

SYNDICATES A point to low-ball on each hole. If low-ball is tied by two or more players, no point is won, even though remaining member or members of foursome took many more strokes.

CUMULATIVE SYNDICATES Same as above, except that points not won on tied holes carry forward and go to the first player to win a low-ball. Thus a player may not have been a party to the tying on two consecutive holes, yet on the third hole have low-ball and thus win the points of all three holes.

SYNDICATE TOURNEY Played with full handicap. Golfers post their scores, then put a ring around their score on each hole where they are entitled to a stroke by their handicap. This is to aid the committee, who looks over the scores of the entire field and picks the man whose net score is lowest for the first hole. If no one has tied him, he wins the hole from the entire field and wins 1/18th of the prize money. If two or more players tie for low on the first hole, the committee examines the second hole, and so on, until a hole is reached where one golfer has a clear net win. Tied holes carry forward to next win hole. Suggested entry: 5¢ per hole (90¢). On eighteenth hole, if no syndicate is won, tying low players split whatever entry money remains.

TEAM MATCH—NASSAU SYSTEM Regular 18 hole matches are played by two or more teams, but the scoring is on the Nassau System basis— 1 point for the first 9 holes and 1 point for the second 9 holes and 1 point for the match. This is a good method of scoring in that it gives a player a chance to salvage something after he may have had a very bad start.

THREE-BALL MATCHES In this match three players play together. Each may play against both of the others, or where one player is better than either of the other two he will play against the best ball of the two poorer players.

ONE-HALF AGGREGATE SCORE This is a variation of the above described Three-Ball Match and is used where the players are of equal playing ability and one of them is not enough better than the other two to justify his playing their best ball. In this case the scores of the two partners are added and one-half thereof counts against the odd player's score. For example, one of the partners takes a four and the other a three, making a total of seven, their score for the hole being 3½. The odd player must beat this in order to win.

THREESOME MATCH One player, hitting every shot, opposes two players who stroke alternately at a single ball. A traditional event in the British Isles, this contest does not seem to have much popularity this side of the ocean.

THROW-OUT TOURNEY Medal play, full handicap. Each player may throw out his three worst holes, i.e., only 15 holes are counted in determining net scores.

TIN WHISTLE TOURNAMENT This competition is on a match play basis and points are awarded as follows:

1 point for each hole made in 1 over par, 3 points for par, 5 points for each birdie.

The player having the greatest number of points at the end of the round wins.

This is played on a handicap basis and strokes are taken at the hole specified on the score card. A par scored, less a handicap stroke, counts as a birdie.

TURKEY TOURNAMENT This event is played the same as a Kicker's Handicap, except that a turkey is awarded to each of three winners.

A small entry fee may be charged to cover the cost of the turkeys.

TWO-BALL FOURSOME Two players constitute a team and one ball only is used by each team, the partners alternate in playing the shots. One partner drives from all the even numbered tees and the other partner drives from all the odd numbered tees regardless of which one made the last stroke on the previous hole. If this event is played on a handicap basis, one-half of the combined handicaps is used.

WHITE ELEPHANT TOURNAMENT Each contestant brings some useful article that he is willing to give as an entry fee. This article is to be all wrapped up and a number attached to it starting with No. 1 and running up to as high as there are entries.

Play is on a low net basis and the winner receives package No. 1, 2nd place wins package number 2, etc. In this way each entrant receives a prize.

NOVELTY EVENTS

APPROACHING AND PUTTING CONTEST This is a very popular form of competition for a Sunday or holiday afternoon as it can be played in front of the clubhouse either on the 9th or 18th hole, or both. Each contestant approaches and holes out three balls from 25, 50 and 100 yards off the green. In each case each ball should be played from a different direction. The winner is the one holing out the three balls in the fewest number of strokes.

BLOOPERS TOURNAMENT To qualify for this tournament a player must do one of the following:

Take more than 4 putts on any one hole.

Take more than 4 shots in sand trap.

Take 10 or more strokes on one hole.

Use unnecessary language on at least 9 holes of the round, etc.

As many prizes may be offered as is felt necessary. You may also have a blind bogey between 65 and 75 and between 100 and 110.

"CAN YOU TAKE IT?" TOURNAMENT This tournament is played in foursomes using regular handicaps, and how some of the fussy boys need that handicap after such a hectic round! The idea is to create noise and disturbance throughout the round to disturb and distract your partners. It is advisable to place one practical joker in each foursome to start the fireworks and get the other three members of the party into the right spirit. This is particularly good training for the fussy type of golfer. Contestants are not allowed, however, to interfere with the actual swinging of the club or with the lie or flight of the ball.

Any contestant who cannot take it good-naturedly is fined according to his misbehavior. These fines are set before the match and are applied, when paid, to the tournament fund to buy more prizes for the winners. A crooked-shafted club or badly scuffed golf balls are appropriate booby prizes.

CONSECUTIVE CLUB TOURNEY Each player allowed only four clubs — brassie, 5 iron, 8 iron and putter. All players use the brassie off the first tee, thereafter must use 5 iron, 8 iron and putter in that sequence for all subsequent shots, no matter what the lie of the ball. Player may find himself driving with an 8 iron and putting with a brassie. To even up player ability, allow only half handicaps, so poorer players to whom one club may be almost as good as another, will not run away with the event.

CROSS-COUNTRY TOURNAMENT NO. 1 Start about a mile from the course and play directly across country, finishing on one of the greens of the course near the clubhouse, if possible, but designated in advance. The ball must be played from wherever it lies. If found in an unplayable position, the player is permitted to lift and tee up with the loss of two strokes. This contest furnishes many exciting and unusual situations.

CROSS-COUNTRY TOURNAMENT NO. 2 This contest is played entirely on the golf course, skipping about, however, from one hole to another, not in the usual rotation. Play might start at the first tee and go to hole No. 6 then start at the 7th tee and go to hole No. 14, etc., until at least nine holes have been played.

CROSS-COUNTRY TOURNAMENT NO. 3 Nine holes are enough for this one. Course is not played in usual order; instead, tournament directions supplied each player read something like this:

1st Hole: From 1st tee to 3rd green;
2nd Hole: From 4th tee to 10th green;
3rd Hole: From 11th tee to 7th green; etc.

Played without handicap. Note that the tee to start each hole is the one normally following the green just played, this to save long walks between green and tee.

DRIVING CONTEST Pick a wide-open flat fairway. Each contestant gets five drives, with only the best three counting. Only shots ending in fairway count. For quick determination of distance, erect marker flags each 25 yards from 125 yards to 300 yards. Judges stationed down the fairway, can estimate yardage beyond nearest marker. A variation of this event allows only three drives and deducts 10 per cent from the distance for all shots ending up in the rough.

FORFEIT ROUND This is not for serious play. At each green post directions for a forfeit to be paid during the play of the next hole by the player whose score for the hole just completed is highest. Suggested: (a) Take off shoes and play shots with shoes dangling between arms, laced around neck; (b) Carry all clubs out of bag; (c) Use only putter, tee to green; (d) At the "drink" hole, treat the foursome; (e) Walk backwards, tee to green; (f) Laugh from instant of finishing drive until ball is holed out; (g) Whistle (or sing) from tee to green; (h) Low man, not high scorer, pays penalty prescribed for previous hole; (i) Play all shots standing on one foot. No forfeit is paid on holes where high score is tied.

INCH OR STRING CONTEST Event is played without handicap. Players are given a specified number of inches of string, according to their handicaps, as follows: players with handicaps up to 8 inches get 10 inches of string; those with handicaps between 9 and 15 get 25 inches; handicaps over 15 get 50 inches. These inches of string may be used by the player to call a close-missed putt sunk, or to shift the ball from a bad lie, etc. Low medal score wins. Pieces of string of the required lengths are given to players at the first tee. Knots tell the player how much string he has used.

MONKEY FOURSOME Each member of the foursome carries a single club, those used being generally a wood, a 2 iron, a 5 iron and a putter. One ball is played. Each member of the foursome, in rotation, plays the ball from wherever it happens to lie and with whatever club he has chosen to carry. Thus a player may be forced to putt with a 5 iron, or drive with a putter.

MONKEY FOURSOME, CAPTAIN'S CHOICE Played as above, except each foursome elects a captain who selects the player to make each shot as the strategy of the hole dictates.

PUTTING CONTEST A putting contest is played entirely on a putting course or green. A qualifying round is played and then the qualifiers compete on a match play basis. The whole tournament can be run off in one afternoon. An obstacle putting contest is one where obstacles are placed around the putting green.

OBSTACLE TOURNEY Played with or without handicap. Each hole presents some obstacle, such as a stake off to one side of the fairway that must be played around, or a barrel just short of the green that must be played through.

ONE CLUB EVENT Each player carries only one club, which must be used for all shots. Club may be specified by committee or selected by player. Low net wins. Variation may permit two clubs or even three.

PUTTING TOURNEY An 18 hole event on your practice putting green. Winner determined by total putts. In case of ties, all tying contestants play extra holes at "sudden death"; i.e., player is out on first hole he fails to halve. If club has no practice green, use the "clock" method on one of the regular greens near the clubhouse by marking off 9 "tees" at varying distances around edge of green; each player putts from these 9 tees to cup.

RAZZLE-DAZZLE TOURNAMENT Two teams are picked by the Club Professional from the field of players that shows up on the day of play. A captain is selected by each team. Each team numbers its players from 1, up, with a cardboard pinned on back or chest of each player. Only one ball is played by each team. No. 1 player shoots first, then No. 2, etc., until every player has shot. Then start over again with No. 1. This keeps the entire field of both teams together and many players meet new members they have never met before.

Play with regular Razzle-dazzle rules, i.e., make all the noise you want, at any time you want to razz the opposing team, without touching them.

SHIMBY-SHAMBY Holes are cut in various shapes and sizes, and located in out-of-the-ordinary spots on the greens — in a corner, on a steep ridge, etc. On the tees, the markers are not placed to make the problems of the golfers any easier. Anything goes by way of noise, by mouth, horns or bells, and a player can dance and tease while another is making his shot. Contestants are not permitted, however, to interfere with the actual swinging of the club or alter the lie of a ball. Not an event for a fussy golfer.

SOLO-CLUB TEAM MATCH Two teams, each with twelve men and a non-playing captain, are chosen. The players are numbered and each player uses only the club assigned to him as follows:

Player No. 1 uses Driver
Player No. 2 uses Brassie
Player No. 3 uses Spoon
Player No. 4 uses No. 2 Iron
Player No. 5 uses No. 3 Iron
Player No. 6 uses No. 4 Iron
Player No. 7 uses No. 5 Iron
Player No. 8 uses No. 6 Iron
Player No. 9 uses No. 7 Iron
Player No. 10 uses No. 8 Iron
Player No. 11 uses No. 9 Iron or Wedge
Player No. 12 uses Putter

The captain directs the team and decides the club to be used on each shot, the club specified to be used only by the man assigned to it. In other words, each man carries and uses only one club. If desired, a qualifying round may be held to determine the members of the teams, or they may be selected by the committee or the professional.

SWATFEST Entire field starts off first tee together. High man and all ties drop out at each hole. Eventually there will be but one survivor. Be sure each player marks his ball for identification. Don't start this event too late in the day; it is not over as soon as you might think.

TARGET CONTEST Using lime, mark four circles around cup, largest circle with 35' radius, next 25', next 15' and smallest 5'. Establish three tees at distance of 50, 75 and 100 yards from cup. Contestants play one shot from each tee, using club of their choice. Scoring: ball in 35' circle, 1 point; 25' circle, 2 points; 15' circle, 3 points; 5' circle, 5 points; hole-in-one, 25 points.

TOMBSTONE OR FLAG EVENT Players are supplied with small flags or sign markers in the shape of a tombstone suitably inscribed with "John Smith Died Here." As each player completes the number of strokes equaling par of the course, plus his handicap, he leaves his marker wherever his ball lies after the final allotted stroke. Players with strokes left after completing 18 holes, start out again off the first tee, playing until all their strokes are used up. Player advancing his marker the greatest distance is the winner.

DIVIDEND FLAG TOURNEY Variation of Tombstone or Flag Event. Prize is divided among all golfers who hole out on 18th green — whether they have used all their strokes or still have some to spare. This eliminates the chance that one or two players will get 'super-hot' or that they took too much handicap. If no one completes the 18th hole, pay off on all players who hole out on the 17th.